A PASSION FOR LIFE

Fragments of the Face of God

JOAN D. CHITTISTER

with Icons by
ROBERT LENTZ

ORBIS BOOKS
Maryknoll, New York 10545

Acknowledgments:

Excerpts from *Hasidic Anthology* edited by Louis Newman, copyright © 1934 by Charles Scribner's Sons, copyright © 1963 by Schocken Books, Inc.

Excerpts from *Hildegard of Bingen: Mystical Writings* edited and introduced by Fiona Bowie and Oliver Davies with new translations by Robert Carver, introduction and compilation © Fiona Bowie and Oliver Davies 1990, Robert Carver's translations © Robert Carver 1990, published by The Crossroad Publishing Company, New York, and The Society for Promoting Christian Knowledge (SPCK), London, used by permission.

Excerpts from *Hildegard of Bingen's Illuminations* edited by Matthew Fox, copyright © 1985 Bear & Co., Inc., P.O. Box 2860, Santa Fe, NM 87504, used by permission.

Excerpts from *In Solitary Witness* by Gordon Zahn, revised edition published in 1986 by Templegate Publishers, Springfield, IL, used by permission.

Excerpt from *Saint Joan* by Bernard Shaw, published by Penguin Press, New York.

Excerpts from *All Shall Be Well: The Spirituality of Julian of Norwich for Today* by Robert Llewelyn, copyright © 1982 by Robert Llewelyn, published by Paulist Press, Mahwah, N.J., used by permission.

Excerpts from *Julian of Norwich's Showings* translated by Edmund Colledge and James Walsh, copyright © 1978 by the Missionary Sisters of St. Paul the Apostle in New York State, published by Paulist Press, Mahwah, N.J., used by permission.

Excerpts from *New Seeds of Contemplation* by Thomas Merton, copyright © 1961 by The Abbey of Gethsemani, Inc., reprinted by permission of New Directions Publishing Corp, used by permission.

Excerpts from *The Catholic Worker,* 1961, the *Calcutta Conference,* 1967, and *Conjectures of a Guilty Bystander* used by permission of the Merton Legacy Trust.

"No Wall" and "Idle Questions" reprinted with permission of Robert Bly and Coleman Barks, from *Night and Sleep* 1981, published by Yellow Moon Press, P.O. Box 381316, Cambridge, MA 02238. 800-497-4385, used by permission.

Selections from *Open Secret: Versions of Rumi,* published in 1984 by Threshold Books, RD 4, Box 600, Putney, VT 05346, used by permission.

Excerpts from *The Collected Works of Edith Stein, Essays on Woman* translated by Freda Mary Oben, Ph.D., copyright © 1987 Washington Province of Discalced Carmelites, Inc. ICS Publications, 2131 Lincoln Road, N.E., Washington, DC 20002, used by permission.

The Catholic Foreign Mission Society of America (Maryknoll) recruits and trains people for overseas missionary service. Through Orbis Books, Maryknoll aims to foster the international dialogue that is essential to mission. The books published, however, reflect the opinions of their authors and are not meant to represent the official position of the society.

Text copyright © 1996 by Joan Chittister, OSB
Art copyright © 1996 by Robert Lentz

Published by Orbis Books, Maryknoll, NY 10545-0308
Printed in Italy

Queries regarding rights and permissions should be addressed to:
Orbis Books, P.O. Box 308, Maryknoll, NY 10545-0308.

ORBIS/ISBN 1-57075-076-9 (cloth)

To Helen Boyle,
a saint of our own times,
who has done more good and made more possible
than anyone will ever know.
With admiration.

CONTENTS

LIST OF ICONS

Acknowledgments

An excursion through time is no small project. It demands, in addition to the normal processes of the writer's craft, the heart of a critic and the breadth of a historian. In this book, I have been given unmerited and immeasurable help in all of these aspects.

In order to determine the relevance and meaning of each of the figures to our own time, I developed a seminar of researchers and reactors from my own Benedictine community, each of them familiar with the history of spirituality and each of them prepared in special disciplines and engaged in contemporary ministries. Their task was to submit to the seminar background information on a particular character with particular concern for that person's relationship to the issues and challenges of our own day. If the seminar concluded that a particular person had meaning for our time, we gave that figure special consideration. Not all of the personalities covered were included in the final manuscript. The size of the published book was a limiting factor for obvious reasons.

Nevertheless, each discussion affected the ones before and after it. In my mind, none of the concerns or insights were lost. Even if a particular personage was not included in the final outline, the insights from one personage illuminated the presentation of a dozen others.

There is no end, therefore, to my gratitude to the participants in that seminar: Audrey Berdis, OSB, Marlene Bertke, OSB, Marcie Bircher, Margarita Dangel, OSB, Susan Freitag, OSB, Therese Glass, OSB, Mary Grace Hanes, OSB, Christine Kosin, OSB, Karen Kosin OSB, Mary Lou Kownacki, OSB, Rosanne Lindal-Hynes, OSB, Irene Lucas, OSB, Mary Ann Luke, OSB, Mary Miller, OSB, Ann Muczynski, OSB, Elizabeth Oettel, OSB, Mary Ellen Plumb, OSB, Catherine Rettger, OSB, Dianne Sabol, OSB, Marilyn Schauble, OSB, Stephanie Schmidt, OSB, Claire Marie Surmik, OSB, Lucia Surmik, OSB, Maureen Tobin, OSB, Judith Trambley, OSB, Margaret Wehrer, Barbara Wojciak, OSB, Charlotte Zalot, OSB, and Margaret Zeller, OSB. Without them, this book could never have been completed.

As usual, I am deeply indebted to those readers who brought criticism and technical expertise to the final text: Marlene Bertke, OSB, Stephanie Campbell, OSB, Mary Lou Kownacki, OSB, Barbara Wojciak, OSB, and Diane Wilson.

I am warmly and especially grateful to Dr. William Hickey, president of St. Mary's College, Notre Dame, Indiana, and Dr. Keith Egan, director of the Center for Spirituality there under whose aegis I functioned as Scholar-in-Residence while writing this book. They gave me the resources, the time, and the space I needed to do it. More than that, they gave me personal support and encouragement.

In addition, I remember with a loving smile Sr. Bernice Hollenhorst, CSC, and the staff of

St. Mary's library, who never missed on a single reference, who took me in as one of themselves, who broke library rules in my behalf with a cavalier kind of attitude that makes mincemeat out of the standard library stereotypes and leaves me with fond memories enough for a lifetime.

Finally, I am grateful to Robert Lentz, whose icons make these figures breathtakingly timeless and currently powerful, and to Robert Ellsberg, our editor, who envisioned this work, allowed the creative principle to run rampant, and worked with me with patience and sensitivity.

Most of all, I am deeply and personally grateful to the people who supported this work in special ways from beginning to end: Maureen Tobin, OSB, who makes my writing life possible while the rest of life goes on; Mary Grace Hanes, OSB, who does the work that makes the writing readable; Marlene Bertke, OSB, and Barbara Wojciak, OSB, who allow not a jot or a tittle of the manuscript to go by unnoted. To them no gratitude can be adequately expressed or ever repaid.

To all of you, my great respect.

Introduction

At its best, life is a confusing complex of truths in tension. What work demands of us often diminishes home life. What governments call legal, the church sometimes calls immoral. What conscience requires, the world regularly calls foolish. What was once called absolute by many is now seen as meaningless by most. Where is the path through such uncertainties? Where is the pool in such cross currents? How do we chart a way through places we have never been before?

Books are popular guides, but books are at best simply collections of ideas to be tried in the hope that what the theoreticians theorize about is really true. Education is important, but education too often provides principles devoid of passion. Discipline is consequential, but discipline often tells us more what not to do than what ought to be done in the face of the unfamiliar.

The problem is that life is more than a series of policies or rules or potential approaches to generic categories. Life is what we meet in the cold, hard decisions of daily living. Life is the struggle between equally imposing alternatives when we are least prepared to choose. Life is what happens to us when we find ourselves in the middle of values in conflict.

At times like that, there is only one sure place to turn. In times of uncertainty and stress and tension, we look for people like ourselves, reachable figures, who have lived well through situations similar to our own as proof that we too, in all of our smallness, can stretch ourselves to the limits of the best in us.

It is those people with whom this book is concerned.

For centuries the church has confronted the human community with role models of greatness. We call them saints when what we really often mean to say is "icon," "star," "hero," ones so possessed by an internal vision of divine goodness that they give us a glimpse of the face of God in the center of the human. They give us a taste of the possibilities of greatness in ourselves.

Two things have happened to the modern notion of saint, however: first, saints have become official; second, saints have become bland.

In the fourteenth century, after hundreds of years of identification of saints by popular acclaim, the Vatican developed a process and criteria to determine if the persons venerated by a local population were worthy of general emulation. The canonization process, for the most part, had both substance and merit. The proliferation of local saints by the people who knew them or were impressed by the fruits of their spirituality or the value of their works was a grand and perceptive gesture. If nothing else, it has something to teach us about becoming aware of the character of those around us. Nevertheless, this redundancy of good served as much to blur the character of greatness as it did to preserve its image. "Saints" sprang up everywhere as every area, every region, every city, every village scrambled for relics and patrons.

At the same time, an officially constructed canonization process separated the people in need of models from the very personalities and forces that had given spirit to their lives in the here and now. In most cases, only those reputations that lasted far beyond the life of the person nominated for sainthood were seen as fit for examination by the Congregation for the Causes of Saints. By that time, of course, their spiritual fame had often waned, their social influence dimmed.

The canonization process looked for the heroic in the good, separated the merely pious from the powerfully holy, wanted miracles as well as the proof of a good life to qualify a person for canonization, concentrated on professional religious figures to the prejudice of lay people and men to the detriment of women, concentrated on ecclesiastical docility as a sign of holiness and judged cases according to the insights of centuries sometimes far removed.

To this day, the process keeps popular hysteria from becoming the norm of holiness. It also runs the risk of reducing holy passion to the level of prosaic piety. It hazards sanctifying the insipid. It chances turning goodness into cardboard. It disqualifies for consideration people who fall in the course of rising to new human heights. It cuts holiness from a common cloth: the theologically proper, the ecclesiastically docile, the morally safe. As a result, it eliminates from regard an entire body of people because of whom the very soul of the world has been stretched but who may not be synchronous with the current ideas of the church, who may not even be Catholic, who may not be without signs of flaw and struggle. It leads, imperceptibly but almost invariably, to a theology of disillusionment, the notion that only the perfect give us glimpses of the face of God — Moses and Abraham, Mary Magdalene and Peter, David and Samson to the contrary.

This book, on the other hand, takes the position that not all those who point the way to God for us may themselves be perfect. There are figures gleaming in their holy causes who are awkward in their personal lives. They are sometimes in confusion, as we are. They are often in struggle with themselves, as we are. They are virtuous beyond telling in one dimension and weak to the point of sin in others. At the same time, they hold a fire in their hearts bright enough to light a way for many. They are impelled by the will of God for humankind and they will brook no less. They stand on gilded stilts above the rest of their generation and become a sign for all generations. They are a proof of possibility from ages past and a symbol of hope for ages yet to come. They stand in mute conviction of the age in which they lived and challenge us to do the same. Most of all, they are important to us now. "One does not help only one's own generation," the Hasidim teach. "Generation after generation, David pours enthusiasm into somber souls; generation after generation, Samson arms weak souls with the strength of heroes."

The central questions of this book are: What qualities will be necessary to live a life of integrity, of holiness, in the twenty-first century? What models of those values, if any, have been raised up to show us the way to God in a world that is more preoccupied with the material than with the spiritual, more self-centered than selfless, more concerned with the mundane than with the divine, more parochial than cosmic? Each of the figures chosen has been selected on the grounds that they have something special to say to us now, in this particular age.

The icons in this book are male and female, Christian and non-Christian, married and unmarried, religious and lay, pragmatists and artists, named saint by a process or proclaimed saint by the people who lived in the shadow of their lives. They are people like you and me. With one exception, perhaps. In their eyes burn the eyes of a God who sees injustice and decries it, sees poverty and condemns it, sees inequality and refuses it, sees wrong and demands that it be set right. These are people for whom the Law above the law is first in their lives. These are people who did not temporize with the evil in one system just because another system could have been worse. These are people who saw themselves clearly as the others' keepers. These are people who gave themselves entirely to the impulses of God for the sake of the world.

The book does not intend to be definitive. In fact, the list of saints is disconcertingly short.

The reader will know a number of other figures who could have been included. What the book does intend to do is to raise up again, through the filter of the present, the lives of those who have lived in circumstances similar to ours and have shown us how to live in them as well, with character, with courage, with passion for the right, the true, and the holy.

The book intends to provoke and provoke, prod and prod with the sight of those whose lives require a critical measure of our own until it becomes clear that sanctity is simply a matter of living for the coming of the reign of God with conscience, with voice, and with authenticity now.

Ἡ ΑΓΙΑ   ἜVΑ

القديسة حوا ـ ام الجميع

EVE
The Image of God

It is hard to imagine anyone who has been scorned more often or rejected more universally than the woman Eve. Men have heaped disdain on her as an enemy of the human race, and women have despised her for the weakness they see in her as having been bred in them as well. And judging from the basic shame that surrounds Eve throughout history, in the art of every people, in the theology of every Christian church, in the hearts of every new and more distant generation, the campaign of derision and contempt has been almost universally successful. The cause of human suffering is the woman Eve, the fundamentalist theology of sin insists, and therefore women in general are to be punished, avoided, controlled, pitied, mocked, and feared. It is a rationale that has kept women out of public arenas, out of intellectual centers, out of ecclesiastical holy places, and out of touch with themselves for eons. That simple theological rationale — that rationale theologized — has kept them down, kept them quiet, kept them in bondage forever. Eve was not to be trusted and neither were they. Eve was out of control and so were they. Eve was a danger to the proper order of society and so were they.

But the picture of Eve the temptress that has served sexism so well for so long is an unkind one to men as well. If woman is by nature a calculating temptress who requires control, then man, who fell to her simpering wiles without a whimper, is, by nature apparently, an unsubstantial, unthinking, sniveling weakling who doesn't qualify to be in charge of anything. If Eve is the enemy who took him down, with a simple, empty-headed, inviting smile, then a man by nature is far too easily duped to be in charge of important things. He is far too embarrassingly gullible; his will power is far too essentially flabby; he is a weakling at the mercy of the weakest of opponents.

The philosophical problem is clear, though it is seldom, if ever, admitted. Either Adam was rebellious and so was Eve, or Eve was weak and so was Adam.

It is not a pretty picture. It does not sound like creation at its best in either case. It does not sound like what scripture means to describe when it reads that "on the seventh day, God made humans, and God said, 'That is good.'"

No, there must be more to Eve than what we have been taught to see or there is far less to Adam, as well, than we have been led to believe.

The fact is that Eve, no less than Adam, is the glory of God; and Adam, no less than Eve, is the sign of humanity becoming human.

The twenty-first century sorely needs a fuller picture of Eve in a world where the loss of respect for the feminine dimension of life has brought us to the brink of human extermination, the most organized brutality in the history of humankind, a control of the goods of the earth that leaves

1

two-thirds of the children of the earth deprived, underdeveloped, and dispossessed and a control over women that brings with it bride burnings in India, clitoridectomies in Africa, exploitative labor practices in the United States, rape hotels in Bosnia, and ecclesiastical invisibility everywhere in the world. Clearly, the human race cannot survive without a commitment to the feminine.

It is Eve that must be reclaimed if humanity is ever to be completely whole, if anything is ever really to change for women, if women in general, not privileged tokens only, are to take their rightful places in the shaping of the world.

We must begin to see Eve for who she is. We must begin to understand that Eve is the graphic memory of the unaccomplished in the human race. More than that, Eve, the other image of God, is the clear picture of what God has not been allowed to be for any and all of us.

The equality of women with men has long been a subject of debate. Women are smaller physically, milder temperamentally, nurturers emotionally, and child-bearers biologically. "And this subordinate purpose," the philosopher Thomas Aquinas taught in the thirteenth century, "affects her negatively and renders her unfit for public activity." To this day, biblical fundamentalists point out that the male was created first and that this primacy is the mark of his superiority—no mention, of course, of the animals that preceded the creation of men. They are quick to note that Eve was derivative, formed out of the side of Adam. And yet, the rendering of the creation of Eve stands in contradiction to all that kind of limited thinking. In Genesis, Adam himself says of her, "Bone of my bone, flesh of my flesh." Someone, in other words, just like Adam himself, someone made out of the same material, someone with the very same substance, someone absolutely identical to himself, someone definitely not to be defined as other, or lesser, or inferior in quality. Eve is the confirmation of the equality of women, not their subordination.

Eve is also our sign of possibility. If women are made of the same fabric as men, then women, too, are normative and unlimited in human potential. Eve is full proof that women have both right and reason to expect that humanity with all its blessings as well as its burdens is for them as well as for men. Eve, the one to whose personality apparently Adam succumbed, is also sign to men that it is not brute force that makes a human being strong. It is an amalgam of qualities brought to wholeness that measures the merit of persons and the value of their lives.

Eve is our sign of life in abundance. To both women and men alike Eve is the proof that life can go on, whatever its struggle, whatever its fragility. Eve failed but she did not give up. Eve made a mistake but she did not give in to despair. Eve faced life and kept on going. If anything Eve is a sign to the rest of us that it is in woman that life is kept and carried and brought to fullness, whatever the cost, whatever the struggle to maintain it. It is from women that we get the first glimpse of the fact that, whatever the situation, creation goes on creating. It is through women that we come to realize the down-deep tenacity of life that clings to little and survives. It is not because of weakness, Eve shows us, that life should be reviled. It is because of weakness become indomitable that life must be revered.

It is in Eve that the virtue of hope becomes real. What can be suppressed by the mighty of the world for their convenience and for their ends will be suppressed. But Eve, the other half of humanity, is stark illustration that God will not be controlled, that God will rise in whom God wills, that God is not amenable to human limitations. The fact is that God is often where we refuse to see. God is in those we call ungodly while we make God to our own image and likeness. But Eve is God's proof that God has plans for all of us that will not bow to the chains of those who have no plans for us at all. In women everywhere Eve rises to begin again, full of life, an intelligent, unsung hope for the lowly of the world.

Eve is a sign of the nature of God. First we learn: "We shall make humanity," Genesis states, "in our own image." Then we learn: "Male and female we shall make them." God, clearly, is female as well as male. God is a woman's mind, a woman's sensitivity. God is a woman's body, a woman's understanding. God is a woman's creativity, a woman's sense of values. God is a woman's sense of principles. As long as Eve stands, God's truth stands in all things, too, no matter who chooses to try to repress it in any part of them.

Finally, Eve is the first witness we have to human freedom. It is Eve who, faced with alternatives, was given the right to choose. But choice then, like choice now, has consequences. What could have been easy becomes difficult. What would have been obvious becomes obscure. What would have been guaranteed becomes uncertain for them. But, in it all, Eve becomes an icon of the refreshing frailty of humankind, of humanity struggling to be fully human, of the process of slow growth that brings with it, to those intent on finding it, the wisdom that is born out of an open mind, a wealth of experience, and a thirsty heart. Eve did not sin because she hated life. Eve sinned because she was struggling to live life to the fullest, however confused her perception of the way. Succeed she didn't, we sometimes think, but grow she did, we know, a proof that the human being is capable of learning from errors and may even be intended to learn from errors. Indeed, it is Eve who shows us that by going on through difficulty, through failure, even through sin, we can become even more than we were when we started. A monastic tale tells of the disciple who asked the monk, "What do you do in the monastery?" And the old monastic replied, "Well, we fall and we get up and we fall and we get up and we fall and we get up." Eve, the one whose sights were skewed, is the one God used to prove that the chance to begin again is one of God's greatest graces.

Eve is also a sign to us of how warped we are in our concept of the characteristics of the genders.

It was Adam, after all, who failed to see beyond the present. It was Adam who simply stood by and said nothing while the serpent negotiated with Eve. It was Adam who was dependent and irrational and easily duped. It was Eve who was leader in the lust for life. Nevertheless, given the present punitive reading of what was a common sin, a common punishment, a common call to slow growth and ongoing human development, we have frozen life at its lowest levels — woman the temptress and man the victim. With those icons before our eyes, we have turned men into avengers and women into sex objects. We have called half the human race brutish and the other half a commodity.

As a result, women are the poorest of the poor and doomed to poverty because they cannot get jobs or promotions or wages worth their due. As a result, men are trained to ruthless obedience, to torture in the name of good government and to mass murder in the name of goodness. As a result, women are sold and raped and beaten and burned for dowry money to this very day. And, worst of all, perhaps, they are excluded from the holy-of-holies in churches that call themselves the Houses of God. As a result, there is no end to sexism, no end to giving birth — and to denying birth, as well — to unwanted girl-children, no end to oppression in the name of God.

Eve may, in fact, be the most powerful icon of them all. If the world begins to see Eve as an icon of the feminine in God, then every system will have to change. Every idea will have to bend. Every door will have to open. Every establishment will have to fall. Every negative and limited and manipulated religious teaching about women will have to blush in the sight of God. Every sexist lie will have to give way to the God of Truth.

Eve makes clear that systems based on male power structures and male god-figures are at best only half the ideas that God had for the management of the human race. If Eve is simply a sign of humanity subject to error but certain to grow, then the idea of woman the temptress is as much a commentary on men as it is on women and can never be used again to justify the exclusion of women from seats of male power or centers of male decision-making.

If woman is the undeveloped resource of the Holy Spirit, then no door can be barred to her at the peril of those who already occupy the centers of influence. Establishments that operate without the feminine insight and the feminine dimension of the Godhead proceed at their own risk. They are only limited versions of a human system, at best a whisper of what they could be and should be if God is ever to be fully glorified by us. Religions that build their scriptures and doctrines and sacraments on a false theology of women face the heresy of propagating a false theology of God as well, for they preach a false god, a god who is not both female and male, not pure spirit, but male only — a pathetic caricature of what the God of Life must really be. The icon Eve is stark and continuing proof that truth dies where women are subjected and dominated and oppressed and made invisible and struck dumb. Where women are not both seen and heard, God is only partial, insight is only partial, truth is only partial.

If Eve is an icon of the image of God, then every woman who tries to be heard about nuclearism and, as a woman, is not heard is a dimmed icon of the love of God; every woman who asks for justice and is denied it because she is a woman is a faded icon of the equality of God; every man who recognizes the feminine in himself but represses it in order to protect himself from the machismo around him that passes for manliness is an icon of the God who is hidden by the shroud of sexism; every relationship that depends on the "headship" of maleness is an icon of half a god.

Eve recalls us to our real selves, to our full selves, to our incomplete selves. It is Eve who makes the feminine as normative as the masculine. She makes equality the measure of humanity. She makes us mourn the limitations that we have put upon ourselves in the name of God.

The fact is that Eve is icon of strength and hope, sign and light, star and promise, possibility and opportunity to women around the world, and she challenges each of us to be the same.

GANDHI
The Force of Non-Force

Mohandas Gandhi wrote: "I have only three enemies. My favorite enemy, the one most easily influenced for the better, is the British nation. My second enemy, the Indian people, is far more difficult. But my most formidable opponent is a man named Mohandas K. Gandhi. With him I seem to have very little influence."

The story may be far too familiar to us all. All of us have three enemies; all of us struggle most with the enemy within that is intimidated by the other two.

The situation in India in the time of Mohandas Gandhi was a serious one. The country was under colonial rule. The people were completely disenfranchised and strictly segregated. The country was abysmally poor and without either the political or economic resources to change its circumstances. Britain governed India to fatten its own coffers, not to develop the country itself. There was no doubt that something needed to be done. But Mohandas Gandhi, of all people, hardly seemed the kind of person who would ever attempt to deal with it.

In the first place, Mohandas was a shy child from a traditional family. His father was a chief minister for the maharajah of Porbander who had married Mohandas off by arrangement at the age of thirteen. His mother was a member of the Jainists, a popular Indian religion in which nonviolence and vegetarianism were central, who

modeled a life of private devotions and religious discipline. In the second place, he was a poor student, a stutterer with big ears, who had been the butt of childhood scorn for years and who came out of the experience isolated and afraid to talk in public. Finally, he was not raised a nationalist. On the contrary, he was himself schooled for the establishment. Gandhi became a lawyer, adopted Western ways, began to practice law in South Africa, and earned over $25,000 a year, no small amount for an Indian at the turn of the century. To the most practiced eye, Gandhi seemed well on his way into the system. The British Empire, his first enemy, did not seem to be an enemy at all.

Then things began to happen that changed the shy, docile young man into one of the most visionary leaders of the twentieth century, perhaps of all time.

Gandhi lived from 1869 to 1948, a period that spawned two world wars and the use of the nuclear bomb. He saw raw power unleashed by the powerful against the powerless everywhere. India itself was in its second century of colonial domination with the British Empire at the peak of its wealth and control. In South Africa, where Gandhi took one of his earliest positions, "coloreds" were even more strictly segregated than they were in India. In South Africa there was not even a patina of integration to sweeten the systematic exclusion of a people from their own destiny. One night, Mohandas K. Gandhi,

Ὁ ἍΓΙ Ο͂C   ΜΟ ΓΑΝ ΔΑC ὁ ΓΑΝΔΙ

MOHANDAS GANDHI of INDIA

young, brown, up-and-coming lawyer from India who had accepted the system, worked within the system, upheld the system, and profited from the system, was thrown out of the first-class railroad car. He was thrown off the train by the system in Marizburg, South Africa, in the middle of a cold, cold night because, ticket or no ticket, he was the wrong color for success in that system. He was a human being without full human rights. He was a pawn in what prided itself on being a democratic world.

At that moment, Gandhi made the two decisions that changed the face of the twentieth century. First, he promised himself that he would never use force to win a cause. Second, he promised himself that he would never again yield to force. The basic principles of nonviolent resistance were clear. Now all that was needed was the doing of them.

Gandhi became a community organizer of Indians in South Africa. More important, he became a seeker of truth. *Ahimsa,* respect for all living things, the concept that had been imbedded so deeply in his mother's life, became the ruling force in his own. The Hindu scriptures, the Bhagavad Gita, became his bedrock, his guide. Gandhi immersed himself in an authority above authority and taught others to do the same.

He began to disregard the caste system, to do work that only Untouchables, India's lowest and most despised class of people, were expected to do. He began to discard the symbols of white Western superiority. He gave up all Western clothes; he refused to eat Western foods. He rejected the Western lifestyle. He stopped aping the oppressor in order to bring the oppressed a new appreciation of themselves. He made brownness a holy color. He made God God in a world where everything but God had become the object of its worship.

Then Gandhi discovered that when God becomes God in a person's life, nothing else can be allowed to usurp that place. Gandhi began to

resist anything that did. Gandhi stood up and confronted an oppressive system and found that he was not alone. With a voice to lead them, a path to follow, and a goal to pursue, the oppressed came from every side to join in his nonviolent pursuit of human freedom. And, after years of brutal repression and organizational resistance, a system built for the sake of one people on the backs of another people finally fell to the force of nonviolent confrontation.

In the face of wave after wave of peaceful resisters who refused to bend but who also refused to strike back violently, international public opinion began to turn the tide. Gandhi himself had spent over five years in jail. In the meantime, thousands had been arrested and thousands had been beaten until, finally, the oppressor sickened of its own brutality. England withdrew from the land it could not subdue, beaten by a force that would not fight on military terms. India was free. *Ahimsa* and *satya,* nonviolence and truth, had won the day. Non-cooperation and mass civil disobedience had defeated what no army could have destroyed.

The problem then became that, just as Gandhi knew himself to be his own worst enemy, India became its own worst enemy. Gandhi spent his life trying to teach the eight hundred thousand villages in India to be self-reliant by living simple lives and by learning economic self-sufficiency. He formed *ashrams* everywhere to model and to teach the rudiments of spinning, bee-keeping, pottery, dairy farming, agricultural cooperatives, local self-government, equality, and religious toleration between Hindus and Muslims. But the newly elected government of India simply went on in the footsteps of their British colonizers — Westernizing, industrializing, and modernizing India in ways that left the poor behind and the villages cut off from the prosperity of the cities. The field of the new national politics was a foreign land to religious principles. Finally, after years of civil war, religious toleration failed as well. India was partitioned into two states, India for the Hindus and Pakistan for the Muslims. Gandhi took no part in the celebration. After thirty-two years of sacrifice and work, he watched it all come to ends far distant from what he had wanted. He called himself "a spent bullet," a dreamer whose work for independence had come to "an inglorious end."

His third enemy, himself, was his only clear victory. He had immersed himself totally in God. He had given himself totally to the pursuit of *satya,* the deepest truths of human existence. He had raised *ahimsa,* nonviolence, to the level of the political. He had given the world an entirely new strategy, *satyagraha,* the ability to cling to the truth nonviolently, no matter the cruelty of the kind of pressures against it. He made religious discipline — meditation, fasting, self-control — the raw material of limitless strength. He turned himself and all his weaknesses into a channel of light for others. He became totally pure of heart, the one in whom there was no guile, the *mahatma,* the "great soul" who, loving all the others, lived for them and so became holy himself. His criteria for himself were as high as he had set them for others. "Have I the nonviolence of the brave in me?" he wondered.

> My death alone will show that. If someone killed me and I died with prayer for the assassin on my lips and God's remembrance and consciousness of the living presence in the sanctuary of my heart, then alone would I be said to have the nonviolence of the brave.

He got the opportunity to know, and he passed the test. In January of 1948, as he walked to evening prayer, a right-wing orthodox Hindu who resented Gandhi's compassion for the Muslims, walked up to him, bowed in greeting, and shot him three times. Gandhi fell praying his mantra aloud, "Rama, rama, rama," a plea for the presence of God.

Mahatma Gandhi is a strong, unwavering, white-hot figure whose light has lit many a road. Martin Luther King and the U.S. black power movement walked the way that Gandhi led and brought segregation to an end; César Chávez and the migrant farmworkers walked the way that Gandhi led and made Hispanic farmworkers a power to be reckoned with rather than an invisible minority to be exploited; the peace movement around the world has walked the way that Gandhi led and forced the end of the Vietnam War, the dismantling of the Berlin Wall, the fall of the Marcos regime in the Philippines, and the end of nuclear innocence. He stands before us still, the ghost of peaceful possibilities in a violent world.

Gandhi asks us to critique government and law according to a higher law.

Gandhi reminds us to be patient with others, to do no one harm, to pursue truth with passion.

Gandhi demands that our political involvement and our personal responses be based on a spirituality so deep, a spiritual attunement so constant, a spiritual vision so broad that no personal ambition, no selfish gains, no parochial interests corrupt the depth of our commitment nor the openness of our hearts. No seed ever sees the flower, the Zen teaches. Those who follow Gandhi may, like him, never know their successes. But like Gandhi, too, they will never really know defeat.

Mahatma Gandhi is an icon of the face of the God of Truth, of the God who is relentlessly just.

BENEDICT and SCHOLASTICA
Images of Hope

The story is simple and the story is obscure. A family in the Italian town of Norcia had two children. The boy, Benedict, historians say, was born in the year 480. The birth of the girl, Scholastica, is not dated at all. Some say they were twins. Others question the theory. Whatever the circumstances of their births, he, the *Dialogues* of Gregory say, was sent to school in Rome, an environment so empty and so degenerate that it turned him against public life completely, much as a Plains State boy today might desert Greenwich Village for the simplicity and character of rural life. For Benedict, though, the flight was not simply to a different environment. The flight was to a completely different way of life, to another set of values, to a whole new conception of what was involved in living life at its best. At first Benedict became a hermit in the hills outside of Rome. Eventually he became founding abbot of a series of monasteries.

Scholastica's turn of direction is unremarked by early historians, but the story told by layers of murals in the ancient hometown church named for her indicates that she may well have been revered by the locals at a far younger age and even perhaps in an earlier era than was Benedict.

9

Her painting is one of the earliest of the frescoes and shows a young and lovely nun. His painting is generations newer than hers and shows a wizened old monk. Whatever the case, Scholastica, like Benedict, was clearly intent on dedicating her life to the pursuit of the life of God, and she too founded monasteries and became an abbatial figure. What is equally clear is that the brother and sister were emotionally close and a spiritual influence on one another till the time of her death.

The ancient *Dialogues* of Gregory, the only source of biographical material that we have on either Benedict or Scholastica, tell us stories in the metaphorical style of the time that give insight into the qualities and character of both of them rather than simple historical detail. Gregory's work outlines the seven miracles of Benedict, and it is in them that we take the measure of the man. Every one of the stories has to do with care for another, not with mystical experiences or esoteric visions or transcendent ecstasies. Benedict, Gregory tells us, repairs a broken plate so that a maidservant will not be punished for being careless; he revives a young monastic who had been crushed under a falling wall while working; he rescues a disciple from drowning; he retrieves from the bottom of the sea the ax-handle of an itinerant laborer, a precious tool without which the man would be doomed to unemployment; he makes the sign of the cross over a cup full of poison and breaks its power; he stops Attila the Hun at the gates of the city and brings peace to the region. Clearly, it is always the human condition that captures his concern, always human need on which Benedict concentrates his spiritual strength. It is not religion for show that interests Benedict. For Benedict the spiritual life is not a way to escape the vagaries of living; it is the way to live life, at its most brutal, at its most simple, to the core.

Gregory tells a story about Scholastica too in a period in which the spiritual power of women may well have been more respected than in our own. In this instance, Gregory writes, Scholas-

tica and Benedict meet for what is apparently a regular spiritual discussion between them. As night approaches, Scholastica begs Benedict to stay with her longer so that they can discuss the spiritual questions of life at greater length than usual. But Benedict refuses on the grounds that it is required for him to return to his monastery before dark. At that point, Scholastica, abbess of a nearby monastery herself, puts her head down and prays intensely until, suddenly, a great storm arises that makes it impossible for Benedict to leave. "My God, Sister, what have you done?" Benedict demands. "I asked you for a favor and you refused," Scholastica answers. "So, I asked my God and was heard." With one sweep Scholastica wipes legalism out of the spiritual life and puts the pursuit of God at its center. With one gesture, Scholastica, an Elijah figure, a rainmaker, becomes the spiritual guide of the great spiritual guide and demonstrates for all of us at the same time that God, not custom, no matter how revered, must really be the criterion upon which we base our life decisions.

The stories are fanciful to modern ears, perhaps, but logical to the heart. These are the things of which humanity is made: the spiritual life and human community. As a result, Benedict and Scholastica do not shine in the human constellation of stars because of who they are as individuals. In fact, no one knows who each of them was as people. No, Benedict and Scholastica stand out in history not because of lives of their own but because of what their lives did for centuries of lives to follow them.

The Rule of Benedict, the legacy of a life lived in common in a fragile and disorganized time, seeded the elements that were later credited with having "saved Western civilization." Now, centuries later, those same elements are needed again. Benedict and Scholastica gave us a completely different way of looking at life, out of sync with the establishment then, out of sync with the establishment now, a glimpse of order in chaos then, a hope for order in chaos now.

The Europe of the sixth century and the West of the twenty-first century, under all the customs and cosmetics of life, are two worlds disconcertingly embroiled. In sixth-century Europe, Rome, an imperial superpower whose roads had united the world and whose armies had kept it under control, was in a state of decline both within and without. The government was sinking under its own corruption. Foreigners were beginning to penetrate the borders with impunity, some silently and some armed for battle. The economy was in a state of total disarray. The tax monies bled from the colonies to sustain the government and support the army virtually ceased as time and distance diminished Roman power and Roman control over the outlying districts. Security broke down everywhere. The unpoliced roads of the empire became the stalking ground of thieves and marauders. Towns and villages were left to fend for themselves in the face of invading Slavic tribes. Patriarchy gave Roman males life-and-death control of everything they possessed — and only men could possess anything. Slavery was a given in a society where to be Roman was to be privileged and to be foreign was to be dominated. "Eat, drink and be merry for tomorrow we die" and "Bread and circuses" — fatalism and hedonism — were the drugs of choice.

It is, indeed, a familiar situation to a contemporary culture that has known world domination bought at the price of human dignity and national defense bought at the price of human services. It is all too clear a situation in a society in which the top 1 percent of the population earns a combined annual income almost equal to that of ten million families in the middle. It is surely a disturbingly similar situation in a society where racism and sexism, only recently the law of the land, are still too covertly present in both state and church, all official documentation to the contrary. It is certainly a familiar situation in a violent society that has taught violence so well that the blood of its children runs in its streets.

Yet, in a totally male, highly militaristic, and class-oriented society, the Rule that Benedict and Scholastica passed on to future generations modeled three major feminine qualities that turned the world around: community, obedience, and humility.

Benedict and Scholastica are icons of the human face of God.

The Rule of Benedict does not require great individual asceticism. The Rule of Benedict requires that people live well together in a culture that used one group for the sake of another, that gave Romans privilege and non-Romans lower place. The monastic communities of Benedict and Scholastica lived a completely different kind of life. "Serve one another," the Rule of Benedict says. "Listen," the Rule says. "Never presume to strike one another," the Rule says. "Let everyone take their place in the community according to the time they entered," the Rule says. The principles are clear. Human community must be based on mutual service, respect, gentleness, and equality. The domination of one sector of society by another, the failure to examine all aspects of every question, the notion that violence can be solved by violence, the attempt to use one group in society for the comfort and convenience of another destroy a society at its roots.

The best that can be salvaged in groups where a few stand on the backs of the many is an uneasy order fraught with tension. In these societies, soldiers pace the streets looking for enemies among their own, governments exist to benefit the rich and repress the poor, the vote gives way to party politics, sexism and racism are givens. In these societies, human rights erode and human life is diminished. But the world as fashioned in the Rule of Benedict eliminates classism, distributes authority, and empowers the weak.

It was of Roman men who were trained to be independent and commandeering and patriarchal that the Rule of Benedict required obedience to the other, to the whole community, as well as to the abbot. "Let them obey one another," the Rule teaches. Let them "put aside their own concerns and abandon their own will." It was not, surely, an easy message for a society trained to govern, expected to domineer.

It is a message of no less impact now than then. The United States expects to domineer in world politics, men expect to govern, institutions expect to do their own will, churches expect people to abandon their own wills, parents and husbands and officials expect to brook no interference, to proceed without question, to give more orders than they tolerate questions. The Rule of Benedict, on the other hand, calls for a society where everyone listens to everyone, where the poor have as much right to govern as the rich, where the insights of women are as valued as the insights of men, where small nations are not used for the development of powerful ones. In the Rule of Benedict, obedience gets turned upside down. The militarism that became confused with holiness in the nineteenth century shows counterfeit here. Here obedience becomes the process of becoming attuned to every voice in the universe, not to the point of confusion but for the purpose of discovering the clarity of God in one another.

Then, in a society predominantly male, decidedly imperial, and corrosively arrogant, the Rule of Benedict counseled humility. And Benedict described what it would look like if we ever saw it. It would involve an awareness of the presence of God in our lives, a sense of creaturehood, a positive attitude toward the twists and turns of life, an acceptance of the adequate instead of a demand for the excellent, a commitment to openness, a reverence for life and for others, a willingness to learn from those around us wiser and holier than we, a gentleness with others and a simplicity of self that shows in the very way we walk. It is strong medicine for those who demand the best and want the most and insist on the power and scorn the other and make themselves their god. But humility could save families and humanize nations and eliminate clericalism and save the planet and stop the decline of the world into militarism.

No one knows much about Benedict and Scholastica as historical individuals, true. But what we do know is that they stood in the midst of a decaying society and refused to go into decay with it. They showed the world a better way to live by living it. They gave hope by hoping. They survived the centuries by refusing to sink to the level of the sin in which the century was mired. They left a legacy to life that confronted every age with a vision beyond its own and lasted far beyond all of them. Benedict and Scholastica are icons of the present face of God.

There is no doubt about it. Community, obedience, and humility could save this civilization again.

CHARLES DE FOUCAULD
Icon of the Universal Brother

I t is hardly the cloth out of which public acclaim is usually made or the pattern for which awards are normally given. Charles de Foucauld was grossly overweight, debauched to an extreme, court-martialed by the military, and a dropout from three Trappist communities. He had been both orphan and social outcast all his life. He graduated 333rd in a class of 386. He had lived with a woman and abandoned her. He was an uninterested and comfortable agnostic. He was by any common standard — military, moral, social, spiritual, or educational — a complete failure, a banal adolescent, a social disappointment. He was indeed the raw material of a human being.

The appeal of de Foucauld's life in a period of drug addiction, religious cults, moral deterioration, educational decline, and social deprivation like our own is that he survived all of it. He dredged up from the inside of him what the culture outside of him was unable to provide: a love for the enemy, a commitment to the spiritual life, a sense of the universal, a spirit of self-discipline, a sense of human obligation. If Charles de Foucauld stands for anything at all, it is the burning magnetism of the presence of God in every human soul that demands the best from each of us.

De Foucauld's greatest gift to the twenty-first century, however, may well be the glimpse he gives us of the universal love of God. De Foucauld went to Algeria at the end of the nineteenth century as a member of a French military regiment to control rebel Muslims in his country's colony and to kill them, if necessary, to maintain the power and pre-eminence of France in its African colony. When he left Africa years later, he had given the world a rare look at the humanity and goodness of the Arab people by living like one of them himself. Like the Christ he followed, he had taken on their humanity, had become one like them, had become the other in the midst of those who were called enemy and infidel by his own people and, in the end, became more human himself in the doing. But it was not easy. Commissioned by the French Geographical Society to do what the French army would not allow him to do, Charles de Foucauld began the exploration of Morocco, intent on seeing it from the perspective of the common people themselves. It was, at best, a noble but a bitter enterprise. De Foucauld never got used to the lice and the fleas and the smells that plagued the lives of the urban poor, but he persisted nevertheless. He had set out to understand these people and he intended to do it from the inside out, not from the academic ivory tower on down.

In the midst of the project, however, de Foucauld discovered much more than the demographic profiles of a strange and largely unknown people. He discovered that the enemy was friend, and that, in the Middle East, hospitality was the sacrament of human community. Slowly but irrevocably, national barriers began to drop away and Charles de Foucauld, archetype of Western decadence and chauvinism, began to transcend the differences defined by the Western world and discover humanity on a global scale.

De Foucauld had wrung one experience out of life after another and found them all wanting. At the same time, he had closed himself to nothing. In the end, it was precisely total emptiness and total openness that conspired to make de Foucauld a man of great spiritual intensity. For years there had been no God in his life at all. "My God, if you exist, let me recognize you," he prayed. But then, after years of search, after years of openness to Islam, which he said allowed him "to sense something much bigger and more true than worldly preoccupations," when he finally did recognize the existence of God in life at the age of twenty-eight, he wrote: "As soon as I believed that there was a God, I understood that I could not do anything other than live for him. My religious vocation dates from the same moment as my faith."

He went from monastery to monastery always looking for the poorest but found no monastery as poor as the people he had lived with in Morocco. The contrast made an indelible impression on him. It was not a religious atmosphere that he was seeking; it was the life of Christ, the life of a poor carpenter from a small town, that Charles de Foucauld wanted to live.

But poverty, his passion, was not his only problem with the monastery. Charles found obedience to a superior extremely difficult. From early on he had wanted to leave the monastery and found a religious order of his own, the Little Brothers, who would imitate the hidden life of Jesus at Nazareth. The idea horrified his spiritual director, and the abbot discouraged it completely. For over seven years, Charles struggled between the two poles of obedience to his inner impulses and obedience to the abbot of the monastery. "Everything within me says that I should give in to my wishes. [But] my father—the superior—tells me to wait....What really keeps me back is obedience." He wrote to his cousin Marie, "It is not that I don't like obedience, but that I don't want to put obedience to men before obedience to God." Eventually the superior general of the order encouraged Charles to follow his impulse. Charles, then thirty-eight, wrote that by that time his soul "was truly sick." Charles de Foucauld was, to say the least, no traditional organization man.

He was ordained, yes, but not to do parish work in Europe nor to transplant it to West Africa. He wanted ordination in order to take the Eucharist to "the lame...the blind...and the poor; to the ten million people [who had] not a single priest." But, then, Charles de Foucauld was seldom conventional about much of anything he did.

In 1901, Charles de Foucauld began to work earnestly against the enslavement of Africans. He wrote bluntly and openly about their situation. They faced, he said, "too much work...a beating every day, no food or clothing, and if they try to get away...they are pursued with guns, and if they are taken alive, they are mutilated....Both their legs are crippled....Almost all of them are children who have been kidnapped...snatched away at the age of five, or ten, or fifteen."

Within three months of his arrival in Beni Abbes on the Moroccan border, Charles wrote to the local bishop asking him to intervene with

Ο ΑΓΙΟΣ · ΚΑΡΟΛΟΣ

CHARLES DE FOUCAULD

Catholic legislators in Parliament on behalf of the slaves. The bishop, in fear of risking government displeasure or even expulsion, cautioned Charles to stay quiet on a subject that was politically troublesome. Better to protect the church, of course, than the slaves. De Foucauld's answer was as straight to the church as it had ever been to the state: It was "regrettable," he wrote back to the bishop, that the "representatives of Jesus are content to defend timidly but never from the rooftops a cause of justice and charity."

Charles de Foucauld never succeeded at much of anything: He never became the model monk. He was much more of a problem to any system than he ever was its joy. He did not begin the religious order he dreamed of starting. That was done much later by people who were inspired by his writings. He did not eradicate slavery in the area. That was done by others long years after his attempts. He did not even please or much impress the church of his time, tucked away as he was in a village of twenty families in the middle of a mountain. He wrote of the place, in fact, "It does not seem possible that there could ever be a garrison, telegraph, or European here, and there will not be a mission for a long time." Therefore, he explains, "I chose this distant spot where I want the only model for my life to be the life of Jesus of Nazareth." No, Charles de Foucauld did not succeed at changing systems. De Foucauld did much more than that.

De Foucauld left a legacy for the twenty-first century that goes far beyond any system.

De Foucauld showed us the face of the hidden God, everywhere in everyone.

De Foucauld gave us another kind of perspective to take into any world that is top-heavy with establishments that work best for the rich and little for the poor, that is full of people who are destitute but ignored, that is geared to build its industries, its politics, and its national pride on enemy-making, and that is committed to the fact that bigger is better, that more is necessary,

and that image is what life is all about. De Foucauld stands in stark contrast to every one of those ideas.

De Foucauld is an icon of the God of the poor and unfamiliar, the rejected and the despised.

It is no small thing to stand outside of establishment life in a world where being part of the establishment is the only thing that merits sure status and assures a clear reward. "Obey us," governments say, "and you will be a valued citizen." "Obey us," the churches say, "and you will achieve salvation." "Obey us," society says, "and you will find acceptance." We know what is best for you. We know what is right. We know what is good, the establishments promise. It is a very seductive kind of goodness, this invitation to let others do our thinking for us. But Charles de Foucauld simply did not follow systems. On the contrary, he tried every one of them and ended up rejecting each of them out of hand. What the army wanted him to kill, he came to respect. What the church wanted him to accept, he came to question. The path that society wanted him to follow held no fascination for him. De Foucauld embraced no system at face value or for its own sake. For Charles de Foucauld, God was above all of them and separate from each of them and never to be identified with any of them. He was free and freed us all.

Charles de Foucauld did not work for the poor. De Foucauld lived with them. He made the life of the poor the substance of his own sanctification. There was no symbolic poverty here. No vows of poverty that assured security. No sometimes almsgiving that dipped in and out of the situation according to the convenience of the giver. No, de Foucauld took on the life of the people he served, "becoming just like them in everything," standing in the midst of their world always as the one who could leave them, but did not.

Why would anyone stay in a predicament such as this? De Foucauld makes the answer clear: because there are so many who cannot simply get up and leave the poverty of their lives, someone has to stay with them so that others for whom the poor are invisible can be made to see them.

"Whatever makes us think," Augustine writes, "that our enemies will do us more harm than our enmity." De Foucauld knew what it was to have our souls twisted by baseless hatred for an unknown other. Trained to control and to kill in order to keep one people under the domination of another, de Foucauld came to deny the necessity of it. He committed the unpardonable social sin of refusing to hate the national enemy; he moved in with them; he called them friend; and, on three separate occasions, he owed his very life to them. De Foucauld's life makes it difficult for any of us to assume too easily that the enemy is really an enemy at all.

Most of all, perhaps, Charles de Foucauld was simply what he was, a poor man who did what he did because he loved everything that God had created. He went where no one was and did good there. He chose to be with people completely unlike himself and become like them. He did not try to erect a system that would save the world. He just set out to save the part of it where he was. He lived a hidden life with major public implications for all of us. The Charles de Foucaulds of the world are really the people who make the world one and the poor beautiful and peace possible. The Charles de Foucaulds of the world are icons of the poor face of God.

THE UNIVERSITY MARTYRS
Icons of the Patience of God

The thing about assassination is that we are so inclined to see it as an isolated event rather than a manifestation of a social climate. We pause over it a bit and then hurry on to other things. We seldom look back at the event unless in purely biographical ways. In fact, we're sorry, in a sense, that we looked in the first place. We're almost embarrassed that we looked, in fact. Assassination seems like such a private indecency. Such a useless indignity of the great. Such a quirk. Such a shame.

The fact is that public assassination is so much more often the unveiling of a prevailing violence, a systemic violence, than it is a sad lapse of social etiquette or a momentary loss of governmental control.

The fact is that assassination destroys some public figures so that we can come to see all the little ones that have already been marked by the system for extermination, one way or the other.

The assassinations of Ignacio Ellacuría, Amando López, Juan Ramón Moreno, Ignacio Martín-Baró, Joaquín López y López, and Segundo Montes, all Jesuit professors at the University of Central America, and the murders of Celina Ramos and her mother, Elba Ramos, their house-

keeper, is just such a situation. These were the ones faithful to the light of Oscar Romero, to the life of the poor in El Salvador, to the call of the church to declare a preferential option for the poor, and to the Gospel of liberation. These were the ones who symbolized the loss of all those thousands of relatively ordinary men and women, priests and nuns, catechists and labor organizers, who had already died in El Salvador's repression and carnage with no powerful people to maintain their memory or who, for at least ten years, had lived lives under siege for thinking differently, or for thinking at all.

Indeed, the problem with the story of the University Martyrs of El Salvador is that it is both an old story and a new one.

The old story is the situation in El Salvador itself. El Salvador, simply put, has too many people, too little land, and nowhere for any of them to go. Cultivation has been extended up the slopes of even active volcanoes with little return for the effort. It is a place furthest from the Good News for the poor. It is a place that mourns for justice.

Into this seething cesspool of inequality stepped the church with its "preferential option for the poor," a far cry from the politics of privilege that had been common to the cathedrals of

SAN SALVADOR 16 XI, 1989

Latin America for centuries. What was worse, the program was spearheaded by priests, nuns, and catechists who worked with the peasant population and who were committed to its development. "Be patriotic," the bumper stickers read. "Kill a priest."

In a social climate of these proportions, the work of the church in its efforts on behalf of the destitute, in its defense of land reform, and in its support of local organizing was soon labeled "the promotion of communism," and the government declared war on the church as well as on the guerrilla movements. In 1977, for instance, a right-wing group threatened to kill all the Jesuits in the country. In 1988, assassins had tried to kill Ignacio Ellacuría the first time. In a nation where church workers were routinely deported or regularly "disappeared," where seventy thousand peasants and organizers had already been brutally murdered to give warning to their peers that social change would not be tolerated, the threat was not to be taken lightly. Even a bishop had been killed in the process, the first since Thomas à Becket, who had died in defense of the church. Oscar Romero, on the other hand, had died in defense of the poor.

The political situation had only grown steadily worse since the days of Romero, however. The United States government kept giving military "aid" and military training to a repressive regime. The Salvadoran peasants kept protesting. The death squads kept killing anyone who spoke out openly in favor of land reform or labor organization. The rebel army launched their largest offensive of the ten-year civil war. This time, ten years after the death of Romero, the people assassinated in retaliation for the offensive were academic types and housekeepers, the thoughtful and the faithful, hardly the stuff of violent public enemies.

Why were they killed? Who were these people? What did they think that was so subversive? Most of all, what does that have to say to the rest of us in a century on the brink of change?

They had to be killed, the military decided, because they were the "brain center" behind the rebel movement. The argument is not true in the organizational sense of the term, but it was not completely false either.

Ignacio Ellacuría, SJ, the rector of the University of Central America, was a fifty-nine-year-old Spanish Jesuit with a Ph.D. in theology who was marked at an early age for a life of reflection and research in the dark libraries and holy halls of academia. Reporters who followed his work say that no milder, less militant a man ever lived. The problem was that somewhere along the way, somewhere in the midst of the stinking barrios and starving segments of El Salvador's mass of impoverished humanity, Ellacuría ceased to believe in the antiseptic and perhaps intellectually immoral concept of a "value-free" education. Ellacuría believed that the function of the university was to be a liberating force in society, to seek the truth about the present world from the perspective of the poor, and then to use that truth to make it better. He said,

> The university is a social reality and a social force, historically marked by what the society is like in which it lives. As a social force, it should enlighten and transform that reality in which it lives and for which it should live.... The university should become incarnate among the poor; it should become science for those who have no science, the clear voice of those who have no voice.

No doubt about it, Ellacuría was a real threat to those who prostituted ideas to the satisfaction of the social system. He wrote a book outlining the electoral fraud in the country and another one criticizing the government's withdrawal of proposed agrarian reforms. He was indeed a dangerous man, if by dangerous you mean someone who is willing to confront whatever is in front of him. And he did, both right and left.

Ignacio Martín-Baró, SJ, the vice-rector of the university, was forty-seven years old. He was a psychologist who used his discipline to study the effects of war on the psyche of a society. Martín-Baró knew that the souls as well as the bodies of the living died in wartime and tried to warn the country and the world of the long-lasting civic costs of social trauma. He wrote in a major psychological journal:

> From a psychosocial perspective, the Salvadoran civil war was marked...by three fundamental characteristics: (1) violence, which directs the best resources of each contestant toward the destruction of its rival; (2) social polarization – that is, the displacement of groups toward opposite extremes, with a resultant rigidification of their respective ideological positions and pressure exerted upon everyone to align himself or herself with "us" or "them," and (3) the institutional lie, involving such effects as distortion of institutions' purposes and ideological screening of social reality.
>
> Each group has presented the other as the incarnation of evil, as "the enemy" that must be eliminated....
>
> Public statements about the national reality, the reporting of violations of human rights, and, above all, the unmasking of the official story, of the institutionalized lie, are considered "subversive" activities – in fact they are, since they subvert the order of the established lie. Thus, we come to the paradox that whoever dares to state the reality or to report abuses becomes by this very act a culprit of justice....
>
> Finally, the militarization of social life can create a progressive militarization of the mind....There is little doubt that the almost compulsive violence, which can dominate interpersonal relations, including the most intimate, and the sociopathic destructiveness manifested by some members or former members of the military forces are intrinsically related to the growing preponderance of military forms of thinking, feeling, and acting in social life. The most serious effect of this psychosocial militarization occurs when it becomes a normal way of being.

The warring factions – the Salvadoran military, the U.S. government, and the rebel forces – all insisted that they were saving society from "communism." Martín-Baró insisted on looking at the death of that society and calling it sin. Indeed, Martín-Baró was a dangerous man who focused the attention of the international social-scientific community on the barbarism going on in El Salvador in the name of peace and order in the Western hemisphere.

Juan Ramón Moreno, SJ, was a fifty-six-year-old ex-high school teacher, novice director, and retreat master who functioned as librarian at the Center for Theological Reflection. He had very limited higher education, but he was a skilled preacher and a teacher of contemporary spirituality, especially to priests and nuns. He collected ideas and grounded social activity in the context of the spiritual life. He was anything but a "radical," a subversive, a guerrilla, or an agitator. He was a sincere Christian looking for a way out of social chaos. He wrote:

> But what is important for our church and for our religious institutes: that the powerful of this world look on us approvingly and support us? Or that we be a cry of hope, good news for the despised of the earth? Jesus' words – "Whoever would save his life will lose it, but whoever loses his life for my sake will find it" – are applicable institutionally to the church and to ourselves.

Clearly, Moreno was dangerous to the old ideas of church privilege.

Amando López, SJ, was a fifty-three-year-old professor of theology, a so-so teacher but an outstanding pastoral minister who brought life, dignity, and hope to the poor with whom he worked in a rural parish. He told an interviewer once:

> We believe in some of the goals of the FMLN [the rebels], but I cannot fight and I cannot tell others to take up arms to fight. But that does not mean that we do not understand the position of those who do. We sometimes talk of leaving, also. But our hope is not in leaving it is here. If I leave, the crisis will stay. Here I may be able to effect change.
>
> We try to work with the government. To let them know that the real route to peace lies with them, not the rebels. We try to tell the United States embassy that if they would not supply the military aid, the Salvadoran government would listen more sensibly to what the people are say-

ing. We try to keep close ties to the government because we believe that they hold the reins of peace.

Obviously, López was a dangerous man because he would not be forced into the kind of rigid social polarization about which the social scientist Martín-Baró had warned.

Segundo Montes, SJ, was a fifty-six-year-old head of the department of sociology and political science who conducted survey after survey of the social situation in El Salvador. As director of the university's Human Rights Institute he alerted the international community to the conditions of refugees and human rights abuses in El Salvador and became a marked man. He said,

> There is a saying — how can we be really free if our brothers and sisters are not free? This is my country, and these people are my people. We here are not just teachers and social scientists. We are also parish priests, and the people need to have the church stay with them in these terrible times — the rich as well as the poor. The rich need to hear from us, just as do the poor. God's grace does not leave, so neither can we.

Montes was a dangerous man. He insisted on unmasking the institutional lie and calling all the forces in society to confront it.

Joaquín López y López, SJ, was the seventy-eight-year-old National Director of "Fe y Alegría," an outreach educational system to enable the poor and one of the early founders of the university itself as a non-Marxist alternative to social change. "Lolo" didn't theorize much. He simply provided systems designed to change life in its present form.

Elba and Celina Ramos, a forty-two-year-old mother and her fifteen-year-old daughter, were peasants. The mother was eking out a living as a domestic in the Jesuit theologate; the daughter was trying to get the education that could lift her out of her parents' level of life. Elba and Celina Ramos were dangerous people. They were the poor. The were the population intent on a better life. They were the generation that was looking for liberation from military repression and U.S. control and oligarchy and destitution. They were the people who had to be repressed.

Who were the University Martyrs of El Salvador? They were people with a purpose. They were academics who believed that ideas could change things and that the Gospel would change things. They were people who thought that doing what they could with what they were would change the world for others.

And what do they have to say to us? Perhaps only this: What are you and I doing with our own simple lives to make life on this planet better for everyone else?

HAGAR
The Abandoned Woman

You see them everywhere, the Hagars of the world. They are the homeless women of every city around the globe, left with children that someone wanted once but have no use for now. They are women condemned to live life far below their abilities. They are the needy women who see other women around them living lives of privilege and of luxury while they struggle simply to survive.

The book of Genesis describes the situation all too well. Hagar was the Egyptian slave girl of the barren Sarah. As mistress, early Semitic legal codes decreed, Sarah had the right to give Hagar to her husband, Abraham, to father an heir and then to claim that child as her own. Hagar was, after all, Sarah's legal property.

The problem, of course, lay in the fact that once Hagar had done her duty to the mistress of the house by bearing a child for the man of the house, she and the child she bore became a threat to the very establishment that had spawned her. The child, Ishmael, became a potential heir to the family promise; the servant girl Hagar, by giving birth to the master's child, automatically claimed higher status in the family hierarchy of wife, concubine, servant or slave. Hagar, simply by doing what her mistress had told her to do, had become a figure to be feared.

In response, Sarah treated her coarsely, and Abraham did nothing to protect her. Desperate, the young girl ran away but, painfully aware of her responsibilities, with no human being to turn to and left with nothing but the consolation of God, finally returned to take her difficult place in life as she knew it.

Things never got better, however. Sarah resented her presence and rejected her son. Sarah, in fact, finally bore her own child. Isaac, this true-born of Sarah and Abraham but begot after Hagar's child, took his place as sole and uncontested heir of the promise. Finally, Hagar and the boy, Ishmael, are driven from the clan to fend for themselves in the unforgiving desert. There, only God hears her cries. Only God sustains her. Only God loves her child.

Our culture is different now, but the parallels are mighty. Society is still full of young women whose place in the system is a necessary but precarious one. The slave-girls of our time do the floors and the dishes and the table waiting and the cleaning for the mighty around them and live on pittances for their trouble. They bear children to satisfy the world's definition of women's role and then are left on their own to provide for those children without welfare monies, without dignity, without help. The men who father the children take no responsibility for them, pass no laws in their favor, provide no support for their welfare, begrudge the tax money it will take to rear them. The well-to-do women of the cities cluck about the shiftlessness of these abandoned ones and chide them to marry well or at least to mother with upper-class grace. The matrons of the towns criticize the arrogance of poor mothers who dare to confront society with children their circle has no intention of feeding or educating or housing.

Like Hagar many of these poor women, alone, lonely, and confused, harbor deep rebellion in their hearts, but few of the elite notice and fewer care. When the nation allocates its resources, there is little doled out for the young women who have been sold into prostitution to support their families in the Philippines or left without job training in the United States. So they live, children at their hip, crowded into bare rooms and working dead-end jobs. They scrape out a precarious living. They never get ahead. They sometimes lose heart. But they go on, attempting to raise their children to slip the bonds of small-ness that have been dealt them by a people who want one kind of servant but another kind of so-cial heir. Loneliness, jealousy, banishment, and invisibility become the plagues that pursue them.

It is then that Hagar becomes a light in the dark-ness, a holy one of God, an icon in the midst of idols. It is in Hagar that the rest of us see the power of dependence on God.

God makes a promise to Hagar as well as to Sarah and Abraham that the child born to her will also have a birthright, will also be a leader of the nation. On Hagar, too, in other words, lies the burden of the future of the world. In God's prom-ise to Hagar, the poor see that the globe is not simply in the hands of the few who control its resources and command its wealth and consort with its beautiful people. The fate of the world is weighed in the balance between rich and poor, between the Hagars and the Sarahs of the world, between those who have more than what they need and those who have little or nothing, be-tween those who direct their own lives and those who live at the fiat of others. The story of Hagar is clear: God has not forgotten Hagar.

God chooses Hagar as one of the four non-Jewish women of the Old Testament who, with Tamar, Rahab, and Ruth, play a role in salvation his-tory. It is so easy to think that the world is in the hands of those who think they control it. At every turn, however, are those who transcend the system and who, by their very distance from it, show it up for what it is. It is the poor of our so-cieties who really show us the fiber of the society. It is the outcasts of a people who show us the real mettle of the people. It is the underclass of a society that is the measure of its upper class.

Finally, Hagar is the foreigner, the outcast woman, the lowest of the low, for whom God intervenes to give us a new insight into God. The fact is that God speaks to Hagar as clearly as God speaks to Abraham. The word of God, it seems, is not reserved for the patriarchs of any order. Women hear the word of God, and women carry it within them. Women are named by God as good, and like Hagar, who called God "One who sees me as I am," women name God as well. Women name God liberator and life-giver and savior in a world that oppresses them, uses up their lives without remorse, and leaves them to the mercy of the unjust and the unkind and the uncaring.

Hagar is the saint of hope and the icon of cer-tainty. She gives us all a new way to look at the world around us, with its classes and laws and absolutes. Impelled by the word of God, she pre-vails over all of them. She allows none of them to thwart her. She confronts each of them with the harsh, unyielding awareness of the will of God. Her sense of God leads to drastic changes in her life, above and beyond what tradition would have prescribed for her. She becomes the outcast com-panion of the living God and gives us all pause in the face of the poor. She raises the question of who is the judge of whom in a world where the manicured and sophisticated assume that God is on their side.

Hagar is a God-follower to an unusual degree. She brings with her a sense of the God who re-sides in the resilient and unbreakable heart of a woman who knows that God has greater plans for her than subservience and suppression. Ha-gar is the saint for those who are tempted to think that God does not care.

RUMI
Icon of Wisdom

It is no small thing to be remembered almost entirely for the ideas and attitudes and insights that we have left behind in life. Some people are remembered for the families they came from; some for the great social deeds they accomplished; some for projects they started. In every case, we remember the factors of life that formed the person as well as the silhouette they cast across our world. Very few are lost in the shadow of their own works. Fewer yet are remembered chiefly for their influence on others. The Sufi saint Jelaluddin Rumi was certainly such a person. All we really know of Rumi, minus a few anecdotes, the barest of biographical sketches, and the usual collection of hagiographical folklore, is what he wrote and what he meant to others.

The biography of Rumi as the world knows it is at best sparse. He was born in 1207 in what is now Afghanistan and grew up in what is now Turkey. He came from a line of scholars, theologians, and lawyers and prepared to be a teacher himself. He led what was for all intents and purposes a very conventional life. And then he met the wandering dervish Shams-i Tabriz, who changed his life entirely and became the human model of the presence of God, the understandable source of his mystical inspirations.

JALAL UD-DIN RUMI of PERSIA

The particulars are few but the meaning is clear: people influence people. People have grave responsibility for one another. Rumi learned how to learn from the holiness of another and then turned that learning into wisdom for others. Great wisdom.

It is one thing to have insight. It is another thing to have power. To bring power to insight is entirely a third. Jelaluddin Rumi had all three.

Rumi was a Sufi, part of the mystical tradition of Islam that calls the Muslim community to be especially conscious of the teachings of the Koran on the transitoriness of life in this world. In its earliest form, Sufism was deeply and rigorously ascetic. The word "Sufism" itself, in fact, is thought to derive from the Arabic word *suf,* for "wool," the kind of garments worn by Islamic ascetics. One thing for sure, Sufism was not an empty attempt at religious devotion. On the contrary. Sufism had emerged in the late seventh and early eighth centuries when the loose living of its ruling classes poisoned Islam with religious mediocrity and public dishonor. In that environment, Sufism became a question mark flung in the name of the tradition against a scandal-scarred sky. Sufism was, in other words, a stream of Islam that emerged as sign to the rest of the Islamic community of the serious nature of God's call and the responsibility of every person to live a holy life.

From its emphasis on spiritual austerity, however, Sufism gradually turned more to concern for the love of God than for the wrath of God. Sufism shifted its concentration eventually from asceticism to mysticism. The woman saint Rabia of Basra, in the ninth century, for instance, called for love of God "for God's own sake," rather than out of fear of hell or hope of heaven. Sufism was not looking for rewards in the next life; Sufism was looking for union with God in this one.

Sufi orders, much like the religious orders of Catholicism in the West, rose rapidly. The dervishes, or *fakirs* — Persian words for beggar

or religious mendicant — lived in monastery-like compounds or spent wandering lives of self-denial. They were Sufi saints in search of mysticism.

The idea is a strange one to the Western mind and its Christian history, though mystics mark the landscape of Western theology as well as of the religious history of the East. The difference is that to the Christian, mysticism is defined as a gratuitous grace of God given to those who deserve it, of course, but nevertheless an unmerited and unpredictable phenomenon. To the Eastern mind, to the Sufi, mysticism was a state of life to be striven for, to be worked at, to be practiced, to be achieved. Jelaluddin Rumi, drawn by the charismatic fervor of the dervish Shams, set out intent on capturing the presence of God in all its glory and speaking it to the world despite the shame that came with the begging that the lifestyle required.

Rumi the poet founded the order of the Whirling Dervishes to symbolize the fevered and untiring search for the Beloved that is the lot of every restless soul who seeks a higher aim in life. Rumi, poet and mystic, the man filled with an overwhelming sense of the presence of God, taught people to dance and whirl to the music of reed pipes — despite the fact that dance and music were normally proscribed in Islam — in order to reach the state of focus and heightened consciousness that made instruction palatable and mystical encounter with God possible. More than that, however, long after the dervishes were a potent symbol in society, Rumi touched every century after him with over three thousand lyric poems about the experience of experiencing God that were designed to lure pedestrian souls one step more beyond the mundane and to encourage more cosmic ones another step deeper into ecstasy. The results are a collection of insights that lend depth to the obvious in life and give light to what is too often obscure.

Rumi left the world a body of poetry that made the human condition a holy one and a corpus of religious wisdom in common language that far surpassed the understandings and teachings of the structures and institutions of the time.

Rumi's poetry dealt with the divine nature of life, the meaning of human love and the reality of union with God. Rumi touched the world with a wand of goodness. He was a poet-mystic, a mystic-poet who both unmasked the God-experience and provided one for generations to come.

Rumi taught in simple terms the philosophy of the ages. He told in simple words the truths of a lifetime. Rumi saw the stuff of human life as the raw material of the divine in each of us.

He said of openness that comes from being centered in the mind of God:

> The clear bead at the center changes everything.
> There are no edges to my loving now.
> I've heard it said, there's a window
> that opens from one mind to another.
> But if there's no wall, there's no need
> for fitting the window, or the latch.

In a world made of false walls between peoples and nations, colors and castes; in churches where God is a commodity controlled by the keepers of the holy doors who have defined themselves into the inner sanctum in order to keep everyone else out; in a society where God is imagined to be outside of life, Rumi's words ring like metal on rock: It's fine to say that we can open windows to the world outside of ourselves, that we can, if we will, let the outside in, but what, asks Rumi, is the point of building walls between us to begin with? The poem is a challenge to face the fundamentals of creation, to take responsibility, to realize that both union with God and human unity itself are both there for the taking.

He wrote of pointless speculation:

> A person hit a Worker a good strong blow from behind.

The Worker swung around to return it; and the man said: "Before you hit me, I have a question for you.
"Now this is it: that sound: was it made by my hand or your neck?"
"The pain I am feeling does not give me leave for speculation. These things are all right to worry about if you're feeling no pain."

The message is stark: While we talk endlessly about the causes of homelessness and the characters of the homeless, the reasons for poverty and the shiftlessness of the poor, the perpetuity of warfare and the powerlessness of the innocent who are warred against, the Worker — the Sufi — knows that pain cannot brook analysis and that analysis is no excuse for refusing to deal with the pain in front of us.

About human freedom in a world intent only on the entrapment of things, Rumi taught:

> Take someone who doesn't keep score,
> who's not looking to be richer, or afraid of losing,
> who has not the slightest interest even
> in their own personality: They're free.

Those words are fresher now than ever, perhaps, as competition at all levels, greed at all depths, and narcissism at all moments becomes the ever-increasing order of the day. In a society that trains its children to win and its young people to live for wealth and its stars to worship their own images, Rumi is a breath of new spirit. To Rumi what is, is enough.

About the sign of the dervish in life, Rumi was clear:

> The Sufi opens his hands to the universe
> and gives away each instant, free.
> Unlike someone who begs on the street for money
>   to survive,
> a dervish begs to give you his life.

The holy ones were not begging, Rumi reminds us, to be a burden. The holy ones beg and throw themselves on our mercy to be a sign to us of our responsibility — our power — in life.

Finally, about the process of union with God, Rumi teaches:

> Dissolver of sugar, dissolve me,
> if this is the time.
> Do it gently with a touch of hand, or a look.
> Every morning I wait at dawn.
> That's when it's happened before.
> Or do it suddenly like an execution.
> How else can I get ready for death?
> You breathe without a body like a spark.
> You grieve, and I begin to feel lighter.
> You keep me away with your arm,
> but the keeping away is pulling me in.

Once immersed in the love of God, once grasped by the presence of God, Rumi implies, there is no meaning to the distance between the human and the divine. After that, life is simply the process of waiting for the gap between what is holy and what is useless to be eternally erased.

Rumi is a poignant voice from the thirteenth century about love and the nature of life and union with God. He is a clear, uncompromising voice to a twenty-first-century world that institutionalizes national hatreds, warps and wrenches and destroys life, makes God in its own image, and casts its sins of sexism and racism and national chauvinism in terms of the will of God. Rumi is a prescient voice who claimed out of the depths of mystical awareness what science proved only centuries later: "First you were mineral, then vegetable, then human. You will be an angel, and you will pass beyond that, too."

Rumi simply never seems to go out of style. He never wears out. He never fails to touch the nerve ends of our lives. In a technological society, he keeps us in touch with the spiritual in each of us. He never stops insisting that the human is the ground of the divine. He is an eye into the human spirit. He is the voice that never quiets within us. He is the dancing disciple in each of us who gives us leave to pursue the higher loves of life with wild abandon. He is a Sufi saint but he is also more than that. He is proof that within each of us lies a vision of reality, a reason for dancing, an understanding of life that supersedes whatever it is around us that is trying to trap us in the mundane and hold us in the particular and drown us in the trivial.

He is the icon of liberating possibility in a world trapped in the limiting and oppressive present. He is the heart of all of us.

JOHN XXIII
A Glimpse of the Heart of God

If you happen to have lived during the papacy of Pope John XXIII, if you were young and impressionable, if you had gone to a Catholic school and held popes next to God, then the impressions you carry in your own mind's eye of this pope may be far more important to the biography of the man than any writer can ever produce. Angelo Giuseppe Roncalli, you see, was more of an event than he was an official figure. In fact, "official figure" may be exactly what John XXIII managed not to be, at least by the reckonings of history and tradition.

He was a smiling barrel of an old man whose eyes watered both with mirth and with love. He roamed around the Vatican looking for all the world like a country pastor in town for the day and out of place in the halls of pomp and power. He had clearly become pope at an age too late to be impressed with it. Nor were people all that impressed with him. He was defined as "an interim pope," a colorless old man who would have a short and ineffectual reign between what would surely be two long ones. The most a baffled world could hope was that he would at best be someone who would be a bridge between the twenty-year papacy of Pius XII and an equally stable administration of whoever would come next, once the world caught its breath and was ready to elect a real pope again.

It was to be a different kind of papacy from what the world had known. What people failed to understand, perhaps, was that Roncalli was a different kind of man as well.

Roncalli was born in 1881; he was made pope in 1958 at the age of seventy-seven. It was hardly a signal of vitality and new beginnings to a world whose systems and consensus on values had been torn by depression, world war, and atomic holocaust. This old man, it seemed, would hardly be up to the unpredictable demands of a new age. And yet, this was a man whose whole life had been spent in a cauldron of change. In fact, whether the world realized it or not at the time, change may have been what John XXIII understood best.

By 1958 secularism, the shift of the center of society away from things sacred to things worldly, was a given. The scientific method of data and proof, experimentation and certainty had cast great question marks on the realms of theology. A technological era that every day brought threat to the life of the entire planet was having a heyday. In the midst of so much science and secularism, churches had not become a nuisance to society; they had become irrelevant to it. The political arena, too, was in a state of turmoil. As the world came to terms with the Nazis,

ἅΓΙ? ΙѠΆΝΝΗϹ
 ὸ
 ΤΗϹ
 ΡѠΜΗϹ

WE ARE NOT ON EARTH TO GUARD A MUSEUM, BUT TO CULTIVATE A FLOURISHING GARDEN OF LIFE.

JOHN XXIII of ROME

communism rose on another side to threaten the social, economic, and theological status quo. It was this world in struggle with itself that had framed Roncalli's life.

It was the time of a church in struggle, too. The old world was long gone by the time Roncalli took an adult place in it. The old church was listing under the weight of a new world too. Ideas about the universe and obedience and truth were in flux; doctrine was in question; old teachings about private morality were remote from new questions about social sin. Not just the world that his predecessor had lived in was gone; the church that Pius XII had shepherded was gone as well.

Old Angelo Roncalli seemed as little likely to function comfortably in the center of changes as momentous as these as anyone could ever be. He came from a poor Italian farm family. He followed a path to priesthood that was basically undistinguished. He kept all the rules and filled all the offices. He was a bureaucrat's dream. On the other hand, however, anyone who looked closely enough could see that the bureaucrat Roncalli had filled each of his offices differently from how they had been filled before him. And that perhaps should have been the clue that this papacy, too, would be anything but business-as-usual.

Early in his clerical career, in 1905, Roncalli received one of the most impacting assignments of his life, an experience that may have marked his own attitudes and actions more than any other single element of his early formation. Roncalli was appointed to be the secretary of the then-new bishop of Bergamo, Maria Rodini-Tedesh. Rodini was a cosmopolitan, a visionary, a hard, hard worker, and, most of all, a man of the people. Roncalli was a bright but essentially simple peasant boy. For the first decade of his priestly life, Rodini showed him the world and its poor. Most of all, he showed him that the Gospel and the church were not incompatible elements. Despite opposition from strong conservative el-

ements in the church, Rodini supported the rights of labor. He spoke out publicly in defense of the workers' right to strike. He founded the League of Women Workers. He supported unmarried mothers. Most significant of all, perhaps, he plunged his young secretary into the center of every struggle. He took the soul of the young priest and turned it into the soul of a serious student of the spiritual life. When Rodini died in 1914, Roncalli appropriated the bishop's purple vestments and, after his own episcopal ordination, wore them for all the major celebrations of his life until the time of his papacy. Clearly, the mantle of Rodini hung heavy and hung forever.

But Roncalli was an even rarer breed than Rodini. He was a scholar as well as an activist, and after a stint as medic in World War I that would turn him against war forever, he began a series of ecclesiastical appointments that seemed to lead him further and further from the crowded hovels of the poor to the mansions of the rich. The only difference was that Roncalli the deftly formed church diplomat insisted on taking Roncalli the simple priest of the people with him. The smile, the presence, the interest in people kept breaking through the pomp and political protocol that went with the office. And, as a result, he broke through decades of distrust and cool indifference as well.

He went from being director of the Propagation of the Faith, where he was credited with having reformed and revitalized it, to being bishop and apostolic visitor to Bulgaria, a country that had little time for either Roman Catholics or popes. Until Roncalli came. Then, the country that had sent only one priest to greet him when he came to assume his office in 1925 said their goodbyes in 1934 in full regalia to a man who, as foreigner and Catholic, had taken on their people, their language, and their politics and whose response to the country at the time of its devastating earthquake in 1928 knew no denominational barriers, no measure.

From Bulgaria, Roncalli went as apostolic delegate to Turkey and to Greece, as unlikely a church diplomat as ever. "If in Rome," the new delegate said, "Christ is a Roman, in Turkey he must become a Turk," and began to learn the Turkish language. In the middle of World War II there, he prevailed upon Turkish authorities to give haven to a boatload of Jewish children from Germany and went so far as to coax the German officer in charge in the region, von Papen, to help Jews escape to safety; Roncalli later testified on his behalf at the Nuremberg trials.

In 1944, he was made papal nuncio to France, where he learned the arts, *haute cuisine,* and the politics of the anti-Catholic de Gaulle.

In 1953 he became patriarch of Venice, the most pastoral assignment of his life, with direct responsibility for a diocese, its priests, and its people. For most men in a similar position it would have been the jewel in the crown of a successful career, a time to settle down, a time to settle in and enjoy. For Roncalli, it was simply prelude. Five years later, in 1958, he became the most ecumenical, pastoral, and politically effective pope of the century. With time against him, the new John XXIII wasted little time reshaping and remaking both the papacy and the church. He held the first audience for the international press corps; he created the first black cardinal; he raised the wages of Vatican workers 25 to 40 percent. On January 25, 1959, John XXIII announced his plans to hold an ecumenical council. Then, on June 3, 1963, only eight months after the opening of the meeting that would change the Roman Catholic Church forever, he died.

His was the five-year-long papacy that changed the world. Somehow neither time nor age nor protocol deterred the man. An ecclesiastical example of the well-trained bureaucrat, he insisted, it seemed, on throwing all the rules away. The stories about his mixture of the very human and the very holy never end. He visited prisons; he picked up people on the streets of Rome and drove them home; he drank wine with workers in the Vatican; he never seemed to take himself all that seriously. "I am Pope John," he said once, "not because of any personal merit but because of an act of God, and God is in everyone of us. I am Pope John and Nikita Khrushchev is Nikita Khrushchev. I don't see why I should think that God shows the truth only through me." And one day in the course of a papal audience with a group of Italian bishops, he spied among them a bishop who had been chief chaplain of the Italian army when Roncalli had been a military chaplain in World War I. The pope strolled among the bishops until he came to the ribboned chest of his past chief chaplain. "Sergeant Roncalli reporting for duty, sir," he said. The remark was more truth than comedy, more the real soul of the man than a posture, more a picture of his memorable human gifts than a mark of his humor.

No doubt about it, Roncalli was obviously efficient, but few remember him for that. He was clearly intelligent, but seldom is he remembered for that. He was undoubtedly politically astute, but only rarely is he remembered for that. What Angelo Roncalli, what Pope John XXIII, is really remembered for is making the political, the scholarly, the efficient, the clerical, and the papal, human. Godlike, even. What stands as his monument is a rare example of a moment in church when the church was open to the world and conscious of its limitations. What stands as his monument is the indictment of ageism by an old man who turned a system upside down to make it new again. What stands as his monument is a bureaucrat's disdain for the bureaucratic. In John XXIII humanity is faced with the need to be human.

What stands as this man's monument is a memorial to the human at its simplest and, therefore, at its best.

HILDEGARD of BINGEN
The Feminine Voice of God

To this day, Eibingen, Germany, and the region around it is a simple place with small, clean houses, a rolling Rhine River that cuts through the hillside, a vast expanse of farmland and vineyards. There is nothing very cosmopolitan here, nothing out of the ordinary, nothing that smacks of the unusual. The place speaks more of the predictable than it does of the atypical. It is a place whose strength is predictable schedules, predictable ideas, predictable people. It is a place, in other words, that is very much like the worlds that most of the rest of us live in. At the same time, it is precisely the arena that spawned one of the most unique personalities in history.

The fact is that, in the case of Hildegard of Bingen, the biographical data simply do not begin to present the person. Her vita, for want of a kinder word, could even be considered dull. Genteel, at least. Proper, certainly. Pious, of course. Hildegard was born in 1098, the tenth child of Hildebert and Mechtilde, members of a noble family in Bermersheim. At the age of eight, her devout parents sent her to a convent as an act of thanksgiving for favors received, a not uncommon gesture of devotion in the Middle Ages when dedicating land and children to God was a demonstration of faith, gratitude, and a spiritual way of life. Having spent her formative years there under the guidance of the wise anchoress

Jutta, she herself eventually became a professed Benedictine nun and, after Jutta's death, Hildegard, Jutta's obvious successor, became abbess of the small community. Then, after sixty-six years of convent life, she died. Period. It was standard-brand development all the way. Except that it wasn't.

Hildegard of Bingen left a legacy that is yet to be inherited by the human race. Hildegard of Bingen became a gauge of excellence that is yet to be universally achieved.

Hildegard of Bingen was knowledgeable, involved, perceptive, committed, and, she said quite clearly, sent by God. She was also a cloistered nun and a woman. The combination is, in most circumstances, even to this day an uneasy one. In this case, it became a banner moment for the church, for the country, for monasticism, and for women.

Hildegard became one of the most influential and widely known figures of twelfth-century Europe. Bishops and kings, priests and scholars, women and men flocked to her monastery from every place on the continent for spiritual direction and conversation. She carried on correspondence with the most important people of the age, with Bernard of Clairvaux, with Thomas à Becket, with Elizabeth of Schonau, with several royal families, with Frederick Barbarossa himself, and with four popes. She scolded priests and castigated kings and warned the vicars of Christ and defied bishops. She was a writer of merit and a speaker of impact. She was a woman instilled with a sense of mission and the pursuit of purpose. She never quit.

Hildegard wrote three major books after the age of forty-two, one on doctrine, one on virtues and behavior, and one on the social situation of the day. At the age of sixty she began the first of four speaking tours of Germany. At the age of eighty-one, almost to her dying breath, she was still speaking and writing. In the last year of her life, in fact, she spent six months under interdict because of a dispute with the local archbishop but preferred to lose the Eucharist and the liturgical prayer life of the community – his punishment for her resistance – rather than give up her passionate devotion to justice.

She was an Olympian kind of figure, a woman whose interests were tied to the agendas of the age but whose spirit was ageless and whose breadth of vision was vast. She knew the major issues of her time – the Crusades, the struggle between the king and the pope, the Cathar heresy – and she spoke to every one of them.

The most interesting thing of all, perhaps, is that eight centuries after her death, she is in the process of being discovered by the world again. Why? The answer may well lie in the fact that she is everything that women and men are at long last discovering women in general to be: inspired, intelligent, fearless, and, indeed, called by God.

Hildegard's inspiration is drawn from her sense of having been personally impelled to record and to proclaim the things that she had come to understand in visions. Commonly called a mystic, she herself made it abundantly clear that she did not receive visual images. She wrote,

> When I was forty-two years and seven months old, a burning light of tremendous brightness coming

from heaven poured into my entire mind. Like a flame that does not burn but enkindles, it inflamed my entire heart and my entire breast, just like the sun that warms an object with its rays.... All of a sudden, I was able to taste of the understanding of the narration of books. I saw the psalter clearly and the evangelists and other Catholic books of the Old and New Testament.

Clearly, Hildegard's visions are intellectual, not sensual. She intuits; she does not see.

> The visions which I saw I did not perceive in dreams nor when asleep nor in a delirium nor with the eyes or ears of the body. I received them when I was awake and looking around with a clear mind, with the inner eyes and ears, in open places according to the will of God.

And then, out of that conviction and under the impulse of the Living Light within her, she explains, "I was forced by a great pressure of pains to manifest what I had seen and heard." She was not, in other words, a nuptial mystic in the tradition of those who lived in ecstasies or practiced rigid asceticisms designed to sustain the mystical life or concentrated only on union with God. Hildegard was profoundly Benedictine in her moderate approach to personal discipline and her commitment to a communal rather than a private spirituality. Hildegard wrote about life in the world, and Hildegard critiqued the world around her from the contemplative's concern for bringing the perspective of the transcendent to the mundane, not from the perspective of a preeminently private and personally intense union with God. Hildegard did not live in ecstasy. She lived very much in the real world, and she demanded that others do so as well.

Clearly, Hildegard is driven by a spirit of understanding to speak a new word to the world around her. And she knows her educational limitations and the social restraints that enveloped her because she was a woman. She writes to Bernard of Clairvaux: "Wretched that I am (and more than wretched in bearing the name of woman) I have seen, ever since I was a child, great miracles."

The greatest miracle of them all, perhaps, was that Hildegard trusted the voice of God within, trusted her insights, trusted her call. She was an intelligent woman who, once she began to produce, simply poured out everything that was in her. She was a scientist, an author, a visionary, a mystic, a prophet, a poet, a dramatist, and a musician whose works are still read, still performed, still sung to this day. In the *Scivias* (*Know God's Ways*), Hildegard explores all the great themes of the Christian life — creation, the sacraments, redemption, the Trinity, eternal life. In the *Book of Life's Merits* she concentrates on the description of the virtuous life, a whole compendium of Christian ethics. In the *Activity of God* and *Causes and Cures,* she presents her understanding of the sciences and medicine that she apparently practiced so well that people attributed to her herbalism a tradition of miraculous cures. She was, in other words, an intellectual phenomenon of the time.

Hildegard teaches, preaches, interprets the scriptures and confronts her world in prophetic fashion with an evaluation of the distance it has come from the will of God. And she did it fearlessly. For centuries, Germany had been a hotbed of feudal wars among the counts, the clergy, and the king, all of whom had their own armies, all of whom were intent on defending or enlarging their titles or their property. A new concept of secular and sacred power was emerging, with the state becoming increasingly more independent of the church, but not entirely, and with bishops often caught between loyalty to the two. The pope still anointed the king as Holy Roman Emperor, and the king had a clear hand in the selection of both bishops and pope. The time was ripe for one conflict after another, one authority in tension with another at all times. The clergy was at least as committed to the temporal realm as it was to the spiritual life; the papacy was politicized, and the king, Frederick Barbarossa, was adamant about the responsibility of the church to swear allegiance to the crown. It was a time of anti-popes chosen by the king in the face of the selections made by cardinal-electors. Hildegard of Bingen confronted every issue.

A prophet they called her as she went from dais to dais calling for the reform of the church and the commitment of the people to the spiritual life. In her own lifetime they compared her to Miriam and Olda, to Hannah and Judith. And like the great prophets Ezekiel and Jeremiah she spoke clearly and fearlessly in the name of God.

She wrote about priests:

> But because they have the power of preaching, imposing penance, and granting absolution, for that reason, they hold us in their grasp like ferocious beasts. Their crimes fall upon us and through them the whole church withers, because they do not proclaim what is just; and they destroy the law like wolves devouring sheep. They are voracious in their drunkenness and they commit copious adulteries, and because of such sins, they judge us without mercy. For they are also plunderers of their congregations, through their avarice, devouring whatever they can; and with their offices they reduce us to poverty and indigence, contaminating both themselves and us. For this reason, let us judge and single them out in a fair trial for they lead us astray.... We should do this so that we are not destroyed.

She wrote to Pope Anastasius IV:

> So it is, O man, that you who sit in the chief seat of the Lord, hold him in contempt when you embrace evil, since you do not reject it but kiss it, by silently tolerating it in depraved men.

Despite her devotion to Bernard of Clairvaux, whose words inspirited the Crusades, she spoke out against the participation of the clergy in the militarism of knighthood:

> How can it be right that the shaven-headed with their robes and chasubles should have more soldiers and more weapons than we do? Surely, too, it is inappropriate for a cleric to be a soldier and a soldier a cleric?

Clearly, Hildegard did not believe in the absolute power of the papacy. In her lifetime she had lived through twelve popes and ten anti-popes. When she denounced King Frederick Barbarossa for his continued attempts to interfere in papal elections, she urged him simply to look to his mission as a Christian ruler. She did not call upon him to submit his temporal power to the pope. The two spheres were separate in her mind, regardless of the ecclesiastical thinking of the day. Obviously, Hildegard was an outspoken and prophetic church reformer long before the period of church reform.

Finally, Hildegard legitimated her knowledge and insisted on the legitimacy of her authority, not by virtue of the permission of men, but by virtue of the nature and plan of God. "Now to the scandal of men," she wrote in the *Vita,* "women are prophesying." And she warned:

> The Word which breathed forth the life of all things...miraculously produced what is written here—not through any teaching of human knowledge, but through the simple and untaught figure of a woman.
>
> Let no one, therefore, be so presumptuous as to add anything to the words of what is written here or take anything away, on pain of being erased from the Book of Life and from all the blessedness under the sun....Whoever presumes to do otherwise sins against the Holy Spirit and will not be forgiven in this world or the next.

Justice was her passion, her impulse. Her writings reek with it and her life was exhausted in its service. Right to the end, she strove against the clergy of the area because of what she saw as an unjust demand. Told to expel from the abbey cemetery the body of a man whom the local clergy called excommunicated, Hildegard herself at the age of eighty erased the markings on the grave to protect the body from banishment and, with the support of her entire community, submitted to interdict with its denial of Eucharist and liturgical chant rather than surrender her commitment to truth. She explained,

> When, a few days after his burial, we were ordered by our superiors to fling him out of the cemetery, I, seized with no little terror at this order, looked to the true light, as is my wont. And, my eyes wakeful, I saw in my soul that, if we followed their command and exposed the corpse, such an expulsion would threaten our home with great danger, like a vast blackness—it would envelop us like a dark cloud that looms before tempests and thunderstorms....So we did not dare expose him...lest we seem to injure Christ's sacraments.

Hildegard was a woman who knew there was a law above the law and adhered to it at any cost, in the face of any opposition, despite any popular concepts to the contrary. She was stubborn, strong, visionary, and ardently prophetic. She was a woman for the twenty-first century who knew that God spoke through women as well as through men. She is the icon of promise for all of us.

Ὁ ἅγιος ΜΑΡΤΙΝΟΣ

7089

HOW LONG WILL JUSTICE BE CRUCIFIED & TRUTH BURIED?

MARTIN LUTHER KING of GEORGIA

MARTIN LUTHER KING
The Icon of Light in Darkness

Scholars have accused him of plagiarism. J. Edgar Hoover tried to destroy his reputation. Politicians called him a communist. Younger members of the black community criticized his passivity. Biographers have lingered long over his sex life.

But the real question remains: So what? Should anyone care? Does it really matter? Certainly those things matter. The question begs for resolution, however: Are these the measure of his contribution to the morality of the human race? The Sufi tell a story about a group of disciples who wanted to make the holy one their guru. When the master declined the honor, the disciples were astounded. "Ah," the elder said. "You don't understand. I am only a finger pointing at the moon. It is the moon you must seek."

The desire to make the sign the thing is a common curse of both disciples and masters alike. It is possible that the burden fell harder on Martin Luther King, Jr., than it does on most. But neither disciples nor guides are served that way, for if we lean too heavily on others for our own direction, leaders lose the freedom to be themselves, and if the leader falls, as fall we are all wont to do, the disciples, disheartened, stand to lose the way. "Strike the shepherd and the sheep will be scattered," the scripture says (Matt. 26:31). But only if the sheep themselves have no sense of the way.

The truth of the matter is that Martin Luther King was Martin Luther King until the day he died — as are we all never more than ourselves perhaps. And yet he was a man converted by the Spirit and filled with holy fire. He struggled with anger and depression and sexual excess all his life. Like the rest of us in our own struggles, he never totally conquered any of them apparently. He saw evil and too deeply abhorred it; he was faced with frustration after frustration and was too often bowed down by it; he lived with human deprivation after deprivation and too often gave in to it. No, King's conversion was not as simple as a change of behavior. His conversion involved something far more difficult than that: King had to find out that God was not only in him but in his enemy as well.

King followed a light, saw a star, felt a pulse, was consumed by a vision that few of us ever see. He may have had to grapple with his own inner discipline, but he was deeply and consistently converted from the "ways things are" to the ways of the Will of God for us, and in his concentration on the things of God he converted us all. Though angry, he was also committed to nonviolence. Though depressed, he was also awash in hope. Though struggling with the pressures of sensuality, he was also loving beyond measure. King knew that sin was not as simple as a lack of personal discipline and that sanctity was not as simple as the gauge of personal control.

Martin Luther King was assassinated at the age of thirty-nine, young by one standard but far too late to destroy what he had begun, not only in this country but throughout the world.

King was an unlikely leader. He was black in a white country. He was a preacher in a world that prefers military men or politicians for the task of leading revolts. He was one of the privileged among the masses of the oppressed. Of all the blacks in the system, King had something to lose by confronting it.

King, after all, had been born on "Sweet Auburn" Street in Atlanta, the foremost residential neighborhood and business center of the African-American community there. He was, in other words, uptown black, the son, grandson, and great-grandson of ministers, a preacher's son who knew respect from his own and a place of privilege in the community. He had a family tradition of proud black men to guide him. He had money and education on his side. He had the ambition to do even more.

But he also had a problem in apartheid-USA and he knew it. Proud as he was of his family and his home, he learned young that he lived in "nigger town," and the sting of it never left him. He lost his two best friends in the first grade because their mother refused to let them play with "a colored boy" anymore, and he hurt from the loss. He had a memory of being called "a little nigger" and slapped by a white woman in a downtown store when he was a child of twelve, and the slap stayed with him forever. He had been with his father when a shoe salesman refused to wait on them unless they moved to back row seats, and Daddy King refused. King wrote: "It was probably the first time I had seen Daddy so furious.... I can remember him muttering: 'I don't care how long I have to live with this system, I am never going to accept it. I'll oppose it until the day I die.'" He grew up abiding "For Whites Only" signs on drinking fountains and public restrooms and elevators and restaurants and barber shops and swimming pools and even in bus station waiting rooms. He knew that the drinking fountains left to him and his kind were dirty and the restrooms

were rank and the elevators were rickety and the restaurants were second class and the barber shops were ill-equipped and the swimming pools were unkept and the bus station waiting rooms were left unclean.

Indeed, Martin Luther King grew up angry. He was nourished by a pre-Civil War church that sang of Exodus while aiding in the escape of black slaves and was inspired by a stream of heroes. Nat Turner, Frederick Douglass, Sojourner Truth, and Harriet Tubman, rebels all, had believed in struggle for change and kept the flame of protest low but glowing in the black community everywhere. Douglass wrote in 1857:

> If there is no struggle, there is no progress. Those who profess to favor freedom and yet deprecate agitation are those who want crops without ploughing up the ground, they want rain without thunder and lightning. They want the ocean without the awful roar of its many waters. This struggle may be a moral one, or it may be a physical one, or it may be both moral and physical, but it must be a struggle. Power concedes nothing without a demand. It never did and it never will.... People may not get all they pay for in this world, but they must certainly pay for all they get. If we are to get free from the oppression and wrongs heaped upon us, we must pay for their removal. We must do this by labor, by suffering, by sacrifice, and if need be, by our lives and the lives of others.

Black women as well had forged their souls in the fray to be free. Sojourner Truth, preacher of peace and prophet for equality, tramped the country to the age of eighty-six proclaiming to white people the sacredness of all life and the equality of women and men. At the time of the Civil War and the contest for emancipation she contended, "Now is the day and the hour for the colored man to save this nation." Harriet Tubman, the ugly, ungainly, ungifted nobody who herself guided slave after slave to freedom in the North, had taught the world that it is in the little people of the land that the power of revolution rumbles most menacingly.

Clearly, King did not invent the conflict for human rights as much as he inherited it. He had, he said, grown up avowing "to hate every white person," but it was not so much hate that he was about as it was confrontation with evil and uncompromise with compromise, his own as well as theirs, his church's as well as his nation's. At the point of enough, King determined to call the conscience of a country that promised in its Pledge of Allegiance "liberty and justice for all" and then systematically denied it to an entire race of its citizens with never even the grace to blush. When the moment of critical mass finally came, he determined to rouse again the spirit of a church that had for too long been satisfied with the ungained gains of the Civil War and that had substituted private pietism for prophetic witness. He determined as well to deal with the anger that scarred his own soul and crippled in him a Christian spirit. How, he had insisted, could he embrace the Christian mandate to love people who hated him? How could he become a minister if ministry meant the passive fundamentalism that he had seen in pastors around him for whom the Exodus, the Sermon on the Mount, the story of Calvary and the resurrection had become more a kind of moral anesthetic used to maintain the system than a call to its conversion?

King found the answer in the social gospel and in the life and work of Mahatma Gandhi, the Indian pacifist who in 1929 had sent a message to American blacks:

> Let not the 12 million Negroes be ashamed of the fact that they are the grandchildren of slaves. There is no dishonor in being slaves. There is dishonor in being slave-owners.... Let us realize that the future is with those who would be truthful, pure and loving.

King set out to seize the future. He learned from Gandhi how to turn anger into positive energy and hatred into love. In 1954, armed with the Gandhian idea of nonviolent resistance, King deliberately chose to begin his pastoral ministry in Montgomery, Alabama, in the center of the segregated society he most disavowed. He was ready to resist, and he did not have long to wait until his whole life would come together and change at the same time.

On December 1, 1955, a tired department store seamstress, Rosa Parks, galvanized the segregated South by refusing to give up her seat in the Negro section of a bus to a white man when the white section became full. It was the arrest of the century. And Martin Luther King, Jr., pastor of one of the major black churches of Montgomery and therefore a natural organization center for the controversy, was ready with the strategy that turned a small minority into a powerful force. King called for a one-day bus boycott, the success of which was so total that King organized it into a 382-day assault on the institutional bastions of white racism — the economy, the political structure, and the entire constabulary system — until they fell.

But King was not simply a strategist. He was a visionary, an idealist, a prophet, a militant Christian, a passionate preacher who articulated for people the very bedrock of faith as well. He said to the thousands of people who turned out for the mass meeting at the Holt Street Baptist Church on the first night of the bus boycott:

> Our method will be that of persuasion, not coercion. We will only say to the people, "Let your conscience be your guide...." Love must be our regulating ideal. Once again we must hear the words of Jesus echoing across the centuries: "Love your enemies, bless them that curse you, and pray for them that despitefully use you." If we fail to do this our protest will end up as a meaningless drama on the stage of history, and its memory will be shrouded with the ugly garments of shame. In spite of the mistreatment that we have confronted we must not become bitter, and end up hating our white brothers. As Booker T. Washington said, "Let no one pull you so low as to make you hate them."

And then King concluded:

> If you will protest courageously, and yet with dignity and Christian love, when the history books are written in future generations, the historians will have to pause and say, "There lived a great

people – a black people – who injected new meaning and dignity into the veins of civilization." This is our challenge and our overwhelming responsibility.

After that, until the day he was assassinated, Martin Luther King waged one long, unending campaign for the soul of the century. He molded the black church into a center for resistance. He targeted one situation after another for black reaction – segregated lunch counters, white educational systems, the labor disputes of black workers, urban housing settlements, voting registration abuses, and finally he focused in on the relationship between business, militarism, and racism everywhere. And he did it all with love of the enemy and passive resistance that changed a nation without leaving a residue of incurable and unforgettable bitterness.

It was an irresistible, irrefutable, and immovable combination. People of conscience everywhere watched their televisions in horror as children were attacked by police dogs and unarmed blacks were clubbed into senselessness and polite marchers were hosed into exhaustion. They saw the brutality of a system that purported to be divinely ordained for the sake of human order. Martin Luther King, Jr., showed us the evil in ourselves, and conscience-struck whites joined courageous blacks everywhere to bring the country back from the brink of its own destruction.

But King paid the price. He struggled constantly with a feeling of inadequacy, a too-young awareness of death, pressures from within the black community, and hysterical hostility from whites. The whole world, it seemed, was conspiring to stop him. He was stabbed three times, physically attacked three more times, bombed in his home three times, and jailed fourteen times before, finally, he was shot to death.

But, in the end, he did not simply save the U.S. black; he saved the very moral fiber of the country and the hope of oppressed peoples everywhere. He changed a nation and gave notice to the world that the powerless are not powerless after all. He left humankind with a higher notion of humanity. He wrote:

> The ultimate measure of a person is not where they stand in moments of comfort and convenience, but where they stand at times of challenge and controversy. The true neighbor will risk position, prestige, and even life for the welfare of others. In dangerous valleys and hazardous pathways, they lift some bruised and beaten others to higher and more noble lives.

King preached, "If a person hasn't found something they will die for, they aren't fit to live." Martin Luther King takes the indifference of all of us and turns it into the stuff of sin. He takes the powerlessness of all of us and turns it into the stuff of strength if we will only pay its price. He casts the shadow of conversion in a new light. Conversion is not so much what we struggle with, perhaps, as it is what we are at our best. If, indeed, as Julian of Norwich says, "Sin is behovable" – necessary, in other words – then Martin Luther King learned his limits so that we could come within the aura of his greatness with confidence and consider it possible for ourselves as well. Martin Luther King's sins became as public as his powerful heart perhaps so that small people like ourselves could feel comfortable in his presence and challenged by his dream. Martin Luther King, Jr., isn't above any of us. He is simply more committed than most of us.

King left us four things: the courage to confront evil square on without the hope of being able to ignore it; the courage to confront ourselves square on without the luxury of despair; the courage to love when hate is more satisfying; and the courage to continue to live until death so that others may have life. Martin Luther King, Jr., gave the humiliated everywhere an icon of pride.

MARY MAGDALENE
Icon of Ministry

For want of a better word, it is at least interesting that one of the strongest women in the Christian scripture is caught in an aura of confusion. What people think they know about her has for centuries overshadowed who she really is. What people expect to see when they look at her, in other words, is what keeps her from being fully seen for what she was in herself then, and what she means to us today.

To clear up the situation at the outset: Mary Magdalene is not "the repentant woman" of scripture. She was not "the woman of the city who was a sinner." The evidence is clear: The same evangelist, Luke, introduces both figures, one in chapter 7 of his Gospel, the other one immediately afterward in chapter 8. For the first woman, the one "who was a sinner," he gives no name and no identification at all. She is simply a woman of the streets, a prostitute probably, who breaks into a male enclave to show them that she is not interested in them at all. She is intent only on the One among them who allows her to be a person rather than a thing.

In the chapter that follows the description of this incident though, in chapter 8, Luke is very specific. In this chapter, Luke is talking about the women disciples of Jesus. The woman introduced in these verses is Mary from the town of Magdala in the Galilee, or Mejdel as it is known today, and she is anything but a woman of the

streets. She is important enough to be identified – an uncommon thing for women in male documents to begin with – and she is mentioned fourteen times. She is mentioned more times, in other words, than any other woman in the New Testament except Mary the mother of Jesus. The woman with the issue of blood, the Syrophoenician woman, the woman of the town, the woman who was bent over, the woman taken in adultery, not even the woman at the well is named. But Mary of Magdala is. And with good reason.

The confusion between the two women, the sinner and the disciple, is an early medieval one attributed to Gregory the Great but repudiated, at least in part, even then. Only in the Latin church was the misidentification widespread. The Greek church, on the other hand, following Origen in his treatment of the two figures in scripture, never collapsed their identity. In the West, however, the teaching of Gregory was buttressed by the renditions of artists who repeatedly put Mary Magdalene into the role of the repentant sinner and the error was seldom, if ever, officially corrected.

In the popular mind, then, Mary Magdalene became the New Testament Eve whose sin had been forgiven but whose character was forever cast in question. As a result of the error, her strength and special calling have been regularly eclipsed. We are inclined to miss, therefore, the prominence given her by Jesus and so the prominence given to women in general, perhaps, in the New Dispensation.

But scripture is very clear. Mary Magdalene is a new kind of woman completely. Mary Magdalene is the woman who becomes the first woman minister. Mary Magdalene is the woman who risks her status in both synagogue and society for the sake of her faith in a Jesus who had confounded both of them. Mary Magdalene is the witness who recognizes Jesus in his earliest moments and stays with him to the end. Mary Magdalene is a leader among the women and a person to be reckoned with by the men. Mary Magdalene is the woman who becomes companion and friend to Jesus and who stands beside him all the way to the cross, next to his mother and next to John, the other one "whom Jesus loved." Mary Magdalene is the woman who is sent to be the disciple of the resurrection to the disciples who had missed it. Mary Magdalene is, indeed, "the apostle to the apostles."

Most tragic of all, perhaps, is that Mary Magdalene, even in the face of such data, is yet the icon of all women clearly called by Jesus to proclaim his resurrection but whose message is ignored. She stands abject in the midst of those who will not listen to the experiences of a woman and recognize in them a challenge to their own spiritual life. Indeed, Mary Magdalene is the woman who sees the Lord and summons others to see him, too. She is a strong woman who did what she had to do to become what she knew she was called to be, in the face of culture, in the face of tradition, in the face of downright scorn.

The situation was not an easy one. It took courage; it took faith; it took a sense of call.

Orthodox Judaism was very clear about the role of women in society. They were to confine themselves to the home or the synagogue except for the sake of domestic duty; they were to be invisible in the public presence of men; they were never to give testimony in a court of law. In pub-

lic matters, in social relationships, and in the professional world they were usually absent, at most ancillary. Mary of Magdala was a sign of contradiction in all three situations.

Scripture says that Mary Magdalene was cured by Jesus of "seven demons," a nervous ailment perhaps, or epilepsy, diseases that were commonly attributed by ancient societies to demonic possession. She was healed by Jesus, in other words, of an inner weakness, of a kind of personal debility, of an inability to function in a balanced and credible way. Thanks to her faith in Jesus Mary Magdalene becomes strong.

The problem is that when the demons go, they all go. The demon of female fragility goes and the demon of invisibility goes and the demon of low self-esteem goes and the demon of fear goes, too. The transformation is a total one. Not only does she become physically hale but she becomes spiritually strong and socially secure at the same time. Mary Magdalene comes face to face with the vision of Jesus and, thanks to him, becomes a new person.

The point is not that Mary Magdalene became a social misfit; the point is that Jesus himself called her to an entirely new role.

Her presentation in scripture is a compelling one: She is called by name, identified by place, and described as a leader of a number of women who supported the work of Jesus "out of their own resources" (Luke 8). She not only "followed Jesus," in public, despite the public prescriptions against it; she made the ministry possible. She saw the truth and determined to set it free. She was not simply a passive listener, a hanger-on. She was a philanthropist of vision, an advocate of godly revolution, a creator of social change. She was part and parcel of the public life of Jesus.

Then, after drawing her profile with broad, bold lines, scripture focuses in on the central reality of Mary Magdalene's ministry: she stayed with him to the end, she witnessed to him in public, and

she became the messenger of the resurrection, when his great, brave, bold male disciples, those who called themselves the apostles, were hiding someplace in the city in a locked-up room.

It is a woman, it is Mary Magdalene, who contends with every system and prevails.

When the others run away from the crucifixion, when the crowds who had welcomed him to Jerusalem within the week had trickled away from the site of the cross, afraid of the authority of the Romans and the disapproval of the high priests as well, it is Mary Magdalene and John who stay with Mary the Mother of Jesus at the foot of the cross while the death of this rebel brings a brilliant three years to a slow and inglorious end.

It is Mary Magdalene who goes with the other women to the tomb to do the customary anointing of the corpse when all the others around him had disassociated themselves from his life, his work, his vision.

She serves to the very end. She witnesses to the last moment. She stands up to face the system when there is no applause and there is no strong support for the movement and there is no protection from its enemies.

Finally, it is Mary Magdalene, the evangelist John details, to whom Jesus appears first after the resurrection. It is Mary Magdalene who is instructed to proclaim the Easter message to the others. It is Mary Magdalene whom Jesus commissions to "tell Peter and the others that I have gone before them into Galilee." It is Mary Magdalene who sees the Risen Christ.

And then, the scripture says pathetically, "But Peter and John and the others did not believe her and they went to the tomb to see for themselves."

It is two thousand years later and little or nothing has changed. The voice of women proclaiming the presence of Christ goes largely unconfirmed. The call of women to minister goes largely unnoted. The commission of women to the church goes largely disdained.

Mary Magdalene is, no doubt about it, an important icon for the twenty-first century.

She calls women to listen for the call of the Christ over the call of the church.

She calls men to listen for the call of the Christ in the messages of women.

She calls women to courage and men to humility.

She calls all of us to faith and fortitude, to unity and universalism, to a Christianity that rises above sexism, a religion that transcends the idolatry of maleness, and a commitment to the things of God that surmounts every obstacle and surpasses every system.

Mary Magdalene is a shining light of hope, a disciple of Christ, a model of the wholeness of life, in a world whose name is despair and in a church whose vision is yet, still, even now, partial.

BARTOLOMÉ DE LAS CASAS
Icon of Justice

Perhaps one of the most telling indicators that we have of the residue of white shame still awash in the world is the fact that so few whites recognize the name of Las Casas at all. He is "Bartolomé who?" in far too many places where his name should be the coin of the realm. In the Bureau for Indian Affairs, for instance. Or in Congress, for instance. Or in the school system of the Western world, for sure. Instead, far too often, he is at best only a wistful memory on Indian reservations, a thorn in legislative assemblies, or an obscure research topic for students of anthropology.

Actually he was a prophet, an activist, and a scourge to the soul.

Bartolomé de las Casas stood alone against a repressive system so massive and so deep that, in the final analysis, he failed at every turn. Yet, ironically, his voice is clearer now than when at first he raised it.

Christopher Columbus wrote in his log about the Arawak Indians who ran to greet his boat on the shores of the Bahamas:

> They...brought us parrots and balls of cotton and spears and many other things, which they exchanged for the glass beads and hawks' bells. They willingly traded everything they owned....They were well-built, with good bodies and handsome features....They do not bear arms, and do not know them, for I showed them a sword, they took

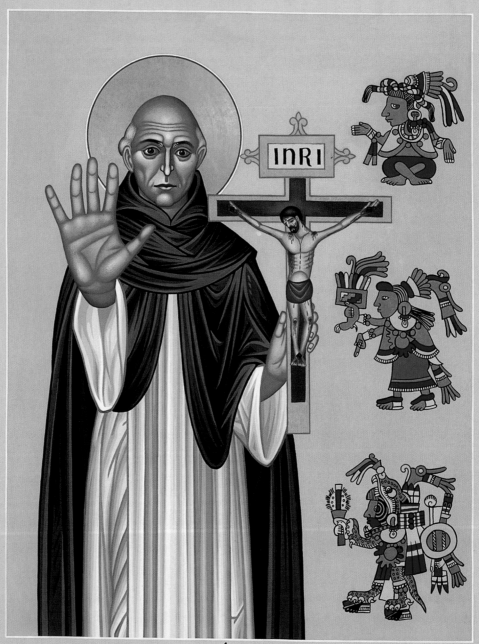

BARTOLOMÉ DE LAS CASAS

it by the edge and cut themselves out of ignorance. They have no iron. Their spears are made of cane.... They would make fine servants.... With fifty men we could subjugate them all and make them do whatever we want.

The whites, it seems, were neither civilized enough to recognize behaviors not based on greed or domination nor civil enough to respond to hospitality and gratuitous sharing with hospitality and sharing of their own. More important, there is still, in many minds around the globe today, the question of whether or not the Western world is really fully civilized yet. As long as the doubt exists, Bartolomé de las Casas will be important to us all.

Historians tell us that the Spaniards attempted to export Indian slaves ("good servants") from the New World to Europe. Columbus and his men alone rounded up fifteen hundred Arawak men, women, and children in the year 1495, put them in pens guarded by Spaniards and dogs and then sent the strongest five hundred to Spain. The problem was that two hundred died en route, and far too many more of them died in captivity. Columbus's only other option, then, since he could not produce the slave population he had promised, was to concentrate on his other commitment to his patrons and fill the holds of the next set of returning ships with gold. In Haiti, they demanded that all Indians fourteen years of age and older collect a defined amount of bullion every three months. Those who did not meet their quota — and Haiti is definitely not gold mining territory — had their hands cut off.

The chief source of information about what happened on the islands after Columbus came is the Dominican friar Bartolomé de las Casas, a linguist, a translator, and a man beyond the vision of the age.

At the age of eight Las Casas had watched Columbus make a proud parade through the streets of Seville on the return from his first voyage to the Indies. Bartolomé's own father, a merchant,

was part of Columbus's second voyage to establish businesses there. And, in 1502, at the age of twenty-eight and before his ordination to the priesthood, the young Las Casas himself went to the New World, apparently as part of his father's business interests, where opportunity beckoned and Christianity was due for a heyday. Finally, in 1513, after two years a priest, he became chaplain to the expedition that conquered Cuba.

Las Casas was obviously not an armchair observer of Spanish Christianity in the New World. He had been part of it at every level. He was the son of a family that profited from the colonization. He was a priest in the church that saw the discovery of New World peoples as an act of God for the glory of the faith and the achievement of the Gospel. No doubt about it: Las Casas saw the New World on every plane. He saw it all. What's more, he says of himself that he cared "more about his possessions and his mines than about the Christian teaching," for he was "just as blind as the secular settlers."

In his *History of the Indies* Las Casas, years later, becomes very explicit about what he began to see when the fog of national chauvinism and the aura of the contemporary theology of conversion began to fade. Spaniards "thought nothing of knifing Indians by tens and twenties and of cutting slices off them to test the sharpness of their blades," he wrote. And in another place he described how "two of these so-called Christians met two Indian boys one day, each carrying a parrot; they took the parrots and for fun beheaded the boys." What was even more appalling, he began to see, was that circumstances such as these were not isolated. He wrote of the mines and plantations:

As for the newly born, they died early because their mothers, overworked and famished, had no milk to nurse them, and for this reason, while I was in Cuba, seven thousand children died in three months. Some mothers even drowned their babies from sheer desperation.... In this way, husbands died in the mines, wives died at work, and children died from lack of milk...and in a short time this land which was so great, so powerful and fertile... was depopulated.... My eyes have seen these acts so foreign to human nature, and now I tremble as I write.

As a result of treatment like that, within two years after the arrival of Columbus, half of the 250,000 Indians on Haiti alone were dead, murdered, mutilated, or driven to suicide. For the Arawaks, all their hospitality had been for nothing; all their sharing of no use.

Historians differ in their conclusions about total numbers of dead, but the estimated depopulation of the Indians after the colonization of the Americas ranges anywhere from four million to twenty-four million depending first on the formulas used to factor in natural causes of death and then on the scope of the territory included in the count. Colonization had become simply a synonym for genocide.

How could any nation orchestrate such barbarity, not to mention one that had embarked on such a great adventure as much for the glory of God, they said, as for the welfare of the rich and the power of the king?

The explanation is, unfortunately, too easy to come by. The fact is that the church itself questioned whether or not Indians were completely human or, in their obvious differences, not some sort of sub-species between animal life and humankind. Theologians of repute argued from Aristotle that some people were meant to be domesticated or enslaved for their own good, not to mention the good of the whites who would do it. It was, after all, the period of the Protestant Reformation and the political impact that the breakdown in Christian unity implied. The thought of building up a new Catholic world while the old one broke down — Luther and Cortés had been born the same year, it must be remembered — was tempting indeed. It was also easy to justify in a nation that had just expelled the Moors and on a continent that had never known religious pluralism.

The question that governed both the spread of the faith and the conduct of the state in regard to the Indians was, of course, their capacity to receive the faith and to live fully human lives. Francisco Ruiz, the Franciscan bishop of Avila, spoke the thoughts of one side:

> Indians are malicious people who are able to think up ways to harm Christians, but they are not capable of natural judgment or of receiving the faith, nor do they have the other virtues required for their conversion and salvation.

The Franciscan provincial Jacobo de Testera enunciated the ideas of another whole group:

> How can anyone say that these people are incapable, when they constructed such impressive buildings, made such subtle creations, were silversmiths, painters, merchants, able in presiding, in speaking, in the exercise of courtesy.... They sing plainsong... they compose music... they preach to the people the sermons we teach them.

The debate raged for decades. The theological discussions were serious ones. In the meantime, of course, the kind of treatment meted out to Indians depended on which side of the discussion a person stood.

Bartolomé de las Casas, once a slaveholder himself who gave up his *encomienda* and freed his slaves, stood firmly on the side of the Indians. He opposed the three pillars upon which the colonial policies of his nation stood: the morality of white racism, the theology of limitation, and the *encomienda* system. What is more, he said so to the very people who were destroying Indians as a matter of faith and a matter of policy. In this commitment to the notion that "all humanity is one," he stood up to the most powerful elements of his society: to the church, to the court, and to the conquistadors.

White racism was built on raw power and new commercial greed. The theology of limitation was grounded in a specious Western interpretation of scripture that taught that God made some human beings superior to other human beings and the rest of humanity their natural slaves. The *encomienda* system became the vehicle for the propagation of both assertions.

The *encomienda* system was designed to populate the Americas and convert the Indians at the same time. *Encomiendas* were tracts of land, plantations — in some cases entire villages — awarded to Spanish settlers by the Crown. Most important of all, however, is that the Indians who lived on the land were part of the package. All the settler had to do to qualify for the land grant was to promise to instruct the natives in the faith for which guarantee they were given, as well, the right to their forced labor. In reality, more Indians were beaten into submission and their heads then counted as Christians than were "instructed" or persuaded of the faith.

Las Casas was himself driven to awareness and conversion by a Franciscan friar who refused absolution to slaveholders and by a sermon of the Dominican preacher Molinas who declared that settlers who practiced "tyranny and cruelty" against the Indians were "all in mortal sin and live and die in it." Las Casas knew the truth when he heard it. He also knew that he had an obligation to bring others to face the issue too. He began to preach against the policy publicly. He began to storm the royal court in Spain with complaints and petitions and recommendations for change in the *encomienda* system. He protested the use of war as a form of evangelization. He made trip after trip back to Europe to engage support for the Indian cause and deter new expeditions of conquest. He spoke and spoke and spoke. He wrote treatises and distributed them. He drew the wrath of churchmen and courtiers alike. Finally, he dared to appear in a public debate with one of the most erudite

scholars in Europe, Juan Ginés de Sepúlveda, who had just completed a translation of the works of Aristotle and so gave great weight to the theory of "natural" classes of people, some slave, some free. Sepúlveda argued that Indians were barbarians who deserved to be punished for their idol worship and whose human sacrifices gave whites the right to wage war against them to force them into the faith. Las Casas answered the arguments with a description of the atrocities of Greek and Roman civilizations whom we respect, a defense of human autonomy in religious matters, and a call to persuade people to the faith rather than to impose it on them.

Finally, after years without success, the world began to listen to this "Defender of the Indians." Finally, Pope Paul III issued the papal bull *Sublimis Deus* in 1532, declaring that Indians were rational, not simply a higher class of monkey or "beasts who talked," as some put it. Finally, in 1542, Charles V promulgated the New Laws that outlawed the enslavement of Indians. Finally, others, both lay and cleric, began to support the notion of universal humanity and the implications of that for the national policies of Christian countries. Finally, the Indian question had become a question of public morality rather than an assumption of power and control.

And who was Bartolomé de las Casas? He was a nobody like you and me who saw a truth and tried to tell it, who saw an obligation and would not quit it, who would not let the question go away, who was persistent to the point of the obnoxious. In a century threatened by ethnic wars, and white minority domination of native peoples, and sexism masked as religion, it may be necessary for us to do the same if Western civilization is ever to come to wholeness.

SIMONE WEIL
Icon of the Face of Truth

She didn't live long enough for us to discover what kind of person, what quality of thinker she would finally have become, but one thing is sure: in the amount of time she had, she lived with more intellectual intensity than most people muster in a much longer lifetime. Simone Weil, a French philosopher, was a fiercely independent, intensely intellectual, profoundly committed, and spiritually centered activist who atomized life, dissected its most minute particles, and synthesized it into a whole again. She spent her life thinking through for the rest of us what few of us would ever think about at all.

Simone Weil was born in France in 1909, at the beginning of a century poised for war and deeply intent on social change at the same time. Society was a steaming, whirling cauldron of ins and outs, of haves and have-nots. The Industrial Revolution had run its course. In the place of its exciting possibilities were now the hard, cold facts of the industrial age. In this world, the wealthy made their commercially successful way through life free of labor laws or taxes or unions or fair labor standard acts. The poor made their living in sweat shops or at day-labor jobs, without benefits, without pensions. People

worked till they died and died from labor that killed them.

In this milieu Simone Weil was a voice crying in the wilderness.

Some people do not go through life easily. Some people are simply not made to live with the unacceptable. Simone Weil was surely one of them. For her, everything was a question demanding an answer, an argument requiring a rebuttal, a conundrum supposing a resolution, an artifice to be unmasked. And she herself was all of them.

Simone Weil was a Jew. In fact, she lost a teaching position in France under the Vichy government for that reason. But Simone Weil never owned her Jewishness. More to the point, she disowned it at every public juncture and the Jews with it. On the other hand, Simone Weil was one of the finest Christian writers of the time, a mystic some would say, except that she never joined the church. She was a fellow traveler with Trotsky and Lenin but never approved of the revolution. The truth is that Simone Weil stood outside of everything she ever touched and critiqued it for the rest of humankind. Nothing, it seems, ever consumed her individualistic self, except the Christ. A philosopher by training, she became one of the major spiritual writers of the time despite the fact that officially she espoused no church at all. Orthodoxy and ritual were not her thing. Life, honest and unadorned, blistering and basic, was the truth she lived for and the path she followed. Her principles were her passion and her passion was principle.

Simone was a brilliant student who graduated from the best of schools at an early age and taught philosophy at various *lycées*. It was not her teaching that distinguished her, however. It was her total and unadulterated commitment to the pursuit of truth that left its mark on her own generation and marked generations to come as well.

Four qualities marked off the life of Simone Weil from the masses around her: rigorous objectivity, ideological independence, commitment to the cause of the poor and oppressed, and religious purism.

Her objectivity cut to the core. Wherever she found pretense, whatever did not ring true, even things she held most dear, she unmasked. A Jew, she rejected the God of the Old Testament; a Christian in everything but baptism, she questioned Christian orthodoxy; a radical leftist, she denounced communism as a betrayer of its own ideals. Even work for the poor, on whose behalf she spoke all her life, she criticized. "Almsgiving," she wrote, "unless it is supernatural, is like a commercial transaction. It is a way of purchasing the victim of misfortune."

Her ideological independence left her without a home in a world of opposites. Weil argued, in the midst of a world drowning in affliction of every kind — war, holocaust, poverty, displacement — that it was only in suffering, only at the break-points of our lives, that God could enter in, not through our achievements and rewards and glories. So though she worked unstintingly to alleviate the effects of evil, she accepted its vic-

tory without yielding to its conquest. She wrote in one of her journals:

> At the bottom of the heart of every human being, from earliest infancy until the tomb, there is something that goes on indomitably expecting, in the teeth of all experience of crimes committed, suffered and witnessed, that good and not evil will be done to her. It is this above all that is sacred in every human being.

A commitment to the poor and oppressed consumed her life and, in the end, cost her the price of death as well. Rather than teach theory about the conditions of the labor force in a depression era, Weil left her teaching position to work with lower-class women in a factory for a year. She journaled every detail of the process and of its effects on her as a person. Frail to begin with, the rigors of the assembly line took an even greater toll on both her body and her spirit. She wrote of it in *Waiting for God*, "There I received forever the mark of a slave, like the branding of the red-hot iron the Romans put on the foreheads of their most despised slaves." Then, in 1943, with France occupied by the Germans, despite the fact that she herself had the opportunity for asylum in New York, Weil insisted on returning to France to be part of the national struggle. In the end, stuck in London, she died a hastened death from tuberculosis because she refused to eat more than the people of France were given at a time when rationing was strict and food supplies were low.

Yet, in those very acts, she lit a lamp for every one of us to follow. Who can be glib, in the face of Simone Weil, about things they do not know? Who can dare to pronounce as fair or just or bearable the plight of the unemployed or the refugees or the women of the world until we have lived their lives and borne their burdens? Who of us can afford to distance ourselves from the sufferings of the suffering around us? Who of us can dare not to listen to those crying for our hearing while the shadow of a Simone Weil, working in a factory, digging in a field, dying a premature death with the workers of the world, sulks over the intellectual landscape of the time?

But above and beyond everything else, Simone Weil was a fundamentally religious person. To the end, she stood outside the church of Rome, refusing to have her intellectual freedom compromised by any system whatsoever. "We must always be prepared to change sides," she wrote in her journal, "like justice – that fugitive from the winning camp." Nevertheless, a sense of the presence of God permeates Weil's relentless attempt to make sense out of life. Private papers published after her death as *Waiting for God* defined her as one of the most important spiritual thinkers of the age. Her commitment to the spiritual questions of the time led her to critique liberalism as well as totalitarianism. Commitment to the individual over the state and individual conscience over group expression was a hallmark of her thinking and grounded in her notions of the sacredness of the person.

Most of all, though, Weil is remembered for her mystical attachment to the personal pursuit of God. Alone all of her life and certain that chastity was the key to freedom, she nevertheless clearly and poignantly describes the encounter with God as the unsuccessful attempt of two lovers to meet in two different places. "Each is there," she writes, "before the time, but each at a different place and they wait and wait and wait. He stands motionless, nailed to the spot for the whole of time. She is distraught and impatient. But alas for her if she gets tired and goes away." Even prayer and meditation she saw as an endless period of

waiting rather than an experience of communion with the divine and prayed at the end of her life to be "insensible to every kind of grief and joy, and incapable of any love for any being or thing, not even for myself."

Simone Weil was a complex and complicated person. She denied her Jewishness, resented her femaleness, forswore her social class. Some saw her as mad, others as maddening. She was, perhaps, a touch of both. It is precisely that, however, that may commend her most to the rationalist in each of us. To those of us who reason without blush that things as they are, are things as they should be, Simone Weil raises a questioning brow. An unchurched Christian, passionate in her devotion to the Christ but skeptical of the church, she is a challenge to center the religious life where it must begin and end, in the God who made us rather than in the institutions that form us.

Simone Weil is a silent invitation to take into the twenty-first century a healthy distrust of everything about it so that no ideology, no institution, no innocent secularism may seduce us into believing that any system is enough for us. She prods us always to ask another question, to want a better life for everyone, to beware the inability to critique our own beliefs and to remember our obligations to make good on our promises. Finally, Simone Weil stands at the center of orthodoxies in conflict as an icon of the search for truth and with a pure eye keeps her focus and ours on the ultimate meaning of things, on the sacred in life, on the mystical in the midst of the mundane.

FRANCIS and CLARE
Holy Madness

The portraits drawn of Francis and Clare are very different from the kind we're accustomed to seeing in our day. In the midst of depictions of the hardened, the tough, the arrogant, the ostentatious, the pornographic, the frazzled, the down-at-the-heels, and the bone weary who populate contemporary society, Francis and Clare are a bucolic contrast. The images that have come down through the ages of Francis of Assisi and Clare, his female counterpart, sitting in the middle of fawning animals or praying before rose-trellised crosses are pictures of total serenity and a kind of contagious bliss. The impressions that the pictures give are both right and wrong.

They are right about the translucence, the transformation of these two people. They are wrong about the environment in which they lived. The thirteenth century was anything but tranquility and roses. It was the period of the Crusades, of urbanization, of the Penitential Movement and of chivalry. It was a period of tension and extremes, politically, socially, and theoretically: the Crusades on one hand, chivalry on the other; old power on one hand, new social classes on the other; unimaginable wealth on one hand, unbearable poverty on the other.

It was not an easy time to be alive. Since the eleventh century Assisi itself had been a center of the foment against feudalism, the basic social institution of the period, but the commune system that followed the feudal estate was no kinder to the poor than serfdom had been and far less secure. War had become a way of life, urbanization a kind of public blight, and turbulence a social norm. In it all, the church that was not only a factor in the wars was also largely rural in its organization. It found itself unprepared to minister in the newly emerging towns with their abject poverty, cycles of unemployment, blatant wealth, mixture of ideas, unauthorized theological opinions, and shifting sense of morality. Giovanni Francesco Bernardone had seen it all.

He had, in fact, been part of it all. He was son of a wealthy merchant, an exuberant party-goer, a rebel, a soldier, a ransomed prisoner of war whose recuperation had been a slow one, and, after that, he was an erstwhile Crusader as well. Little by little, he became a new person with a new vision of life. In Spoleto, where he had gone as part of the papal army, a voice in his dreams spoke clearly:

> "Who can do more for you, the servant or the Lord?" the voice asked.
> "The Lord," Francis answered.
> "Then why are you seeking the servant in place of the Lord?" the voice persisted.
> "What am I to do?" Francis asked.
> "Go back to the place of your birth and through me your vision will have spiritual fulfillment," the voice demanded.
> And Francis returned to Assisi determined to live differently.

It's not an unusual pattern. People commonly go through life changes after surviving major traumas. The distinction in this case is that Francis Bernardone's change of life was an assault on all of life around him, starting with his father's. The break between the father and the son was a violent one. It was also a public one. In his zeal to devote himself to the will of God, Francis sold his father's cloth and horse to get money to rebuild a local church. Pietro was enraged, stalked Francis to the cave in which he was hiding, and locked his own son in a dungeon for the crime. At the town trial before the local bishop, Francis stripped naked in public to symbolize his complete rejection of everything he had once been and announced:

> Listen, all of you, and mark my words. Up to now I have called Pietro Bernardone my father. But because I am resolved to serve God, I return to him the money and the clothes I wore which are his and from now on I will say, "Our Father who art in heaven" and not father Pietro Bernardone.

The picture is very clear. In Francis one generation denies another, one world refuses another, one set of values is abandoned for another, one way of looking at life is challenged by another. Francis saw what Pietro either could not see or did not care about: the poor, the forgotten, the important things of life. Pietro Bernardone was the beginning of the commercial world we now take for granted; Francis Bernardone was its antithesis, its bellwether, its clear-eyed call to social morality. Pietro was one of the self-made men of the new merchant class; Francis was the image of those who had not made it in the system. Pietro was committed to maintaining what he had, whatever it took to do it; Francis was committed to giving things away, whatever it cost to do it. Pietro was on his way up in life to the realms of the rich, to the pinnacles of power; Francis was on his way down in life to the realms of the poor, to the dregs and depths of society where the defenseless can depend in life only on the good will of others.

Pietro wrung wealth out of the social landscape of the time and showed every generation after him how to do the same. But Francis touched the soul of the century and left a sense of conscience behind for the world to contemplate for ages to come. They flocked from across all of Europe to follow this wild vagabond who walked through life with an empty purse and a light step, preaching peace in a warring world and the will of God to a society with a harsh and hardened will of its own.

Chief among his followers was a woman who was a leader in her own right. The young noblewoman Chiara Di Offreduccio, Clare, was an intelligent, educated, and pious young woman. Her own family castle had been sacked during the social upheavals in Assisi. She was well-bred, well-to-do, and meant for the better things of life. When she heard Francis preach, however, she knew that his call to radical poverty was hers as well.

In an age of chivalry, it was a chivalrous relationship. He was her ideal; she was his epitome of the perfect woman. In fact, long after the men who followed Francis had abandoned the purity of his ideals, Clare and the women who followed her continued to embody the ideal of total renunciation in its most rigorous form.

To follow her own special call in life, she took steps unprecedented for women of the time. She rejected her family. After Francis's death, she contested with the men of the Franciscan movement in order to maintain the kind of sacramental and theological contact with the male branch that she felt was necessary to the ongoing spiritual development of a group of cloistered women. She refused special treatment as a woman. She wanted to live the Franciscan life without being subjected to mitigating circumstances. She refused as well the kind of economic "protection" in the form of dowries and property that the church mandated that being a woman required in order to institutionalize the life of penance and total renunciation to which they were committed. She struggled with the pope and his assumptions about what women could and couldn't do in order to get the

СТ. ПР. КЛАРА   СТ. ПР. ФРАНЦІСКЪ

Ἡ ἉΓΊΑ ΚΛΆΡΑ   Ὁ ἍΓ. ΦΡΑΓΚΊΣΚΟ

THE MEETING OF ST. FRANCIS AND ST. CLARE

constitutions she wanted for the women's communities. She threw herself on the providence of God and the sense of obligation to others that cloistered orders without means of support bring to a society by refusing the right for the order to own anything whatsoever, legacies, endowments, or property.

Clare was the one, in other words, who really proved that what Francis talked about was doable for people in general, even pampered upper-class ones.

In the end, Francis and Clare brought five things to the world that shocked all of Europe into a new consciousness and that call to us yet today. They brought a call to peace; a consciousness of the poor; a sign that it is possible to be happy without things; a radical reading of the Gospel of Christ that depoliticizes the meaning of conversion even to this day; and a new sense of the feminine.

The call for peace was a constant. In Spoleto, the archdeacon Tommaso of Spalato wrote of Francis after hearing him speak in Bologna:

> The exclusive aim of all his utterances was to dissolve hatreds and restore peace. His tunic was torn and patched, his appearance pitiful, his countenance unbeautiful, but God endowed his words with such efficacy that many noble families among whom the fury of ancient grudges has been unleashed in torrents of blood became reconciled.

A consciousness of the poor in a society that had long since made them invisible was an essential. Francis and Clare, the wealthy ones who became voluntarily what others had never had the opportunity to choose, put poverty in a new light. Perhaps, the sight of "nice" people in bad situations says to us that maybe, just maybe, the poor are not destined by God to be poor.

Perhaps poverty is not the sign of the inept. Perhaps poverty is not a mark of lack of character. Perhaps poverty is a sinful residue of a sinful system that blames the victim for its victimage. Perhaps poverty is something about which we all have a responsibility.

The presence of a happy pauper in our midst is a very disarming event, a bold attack on everything a consumer society has to teach. If it is really possible to be happy without things then we have to begin to ask what things are all about and what we might be missing because of them. It was after Francis became poor that he began to sing to the sun and talk to the birds and understand the animals and sink into the beauty of nature and kiss the lepers and be fearless in the face of warlords and princes.

The radical among us make us look again at the nature and function of religion and what it does to us and what we do to it. It is so easy to use religion as a way to escape it. It is so much easier to go to church than it is to live the Gospel. In Francis and Clare we see religion for what it is—not as a social nicety, not as a cultural condition of life, not as a political tool for the control of the masses. In Francis and Clare religion stands as stark reminder of the higher life, the whole life, the raw and radical call of Gospel in a church-going world.

The new sense of the feminine willed to the world by Francis and Clare lies in the image of Clare's clear strength and in Francis's commanding gentleness. In these two the world gets a bewitching glimpse of mighty powerlessness.

The legacy of two intrepidly simple people who would not accept life as it was because it could be so much better is as much a gift to the twenty-first century as it was to the thirteenth.

DOROTHY DAY
Icon of the Streets

The thing I have always liked about Dorothy Day is that she was one of the people she dedicated her life to serving. She was not an uptown philanthropist. She was not a nun looking for a good work to do. She was not a government bureaucrat distributing money before getting the commuter train to Long Island.

She was the real thing. She was an unwed mother, a disillusioned citizen, a poor woman, a disaffected churchgoer, an unemployed observer of the human race. She had abandoned the church. She had lived in a tenement of which, as a child, she had been ashamed. She had aborted one child and borne another out of wedlock. She had worked hard to earn nothing and lived in a cheap, vermin-ridden apartment because she couldn't afford anything else. But for the grace of God, Dorothy Day herself could easily have been the Bag Lady of the World par excellence.

She had dropped out of everything worth belonging to, if what you are about in life is credentials.

59

She had dropped out of her family. She had dropped out of college. She had dropped out of capitalism. She had dropped out of churches. She had dropped out of marriage. She had dropped out of the system. She had dropped out of a world marked by all the niceties that finishing schools could provide. Dorothy Day lived in a world of her own. She understood life, she said, out of experience. "I see only too clearly how bad people are. It's my own sins that give me such clarity."

But if Dorothy Day is model of anything at all, it is certainly the fact that life is not over till it's over. What Dorothy Day raised out of the ashes of her life is a monument to living.

It was her conversion to Catholicism — the church of the poor Christ who came "that they may have life and have it more abundantly," the church of immigrants — that gave her the greatest clarity of all. The fact is that, much as she believed in them, causes had failed her. The rise of a new social order in communism inspired her to hope for a better world, but it did not feed her spirit and only too clearly betrayed its own best ideals. A commitment to the elimination of poverty was important but ran aground on the survival-of-the-fittest philosophy of capitalism and gave no insight into the way to deal with those poor for whom rugged individualism was not an answer. Social revolution was a worthy aim but ended in a violence that she had always found suspect. Only when she found "the church of the poor," and "the folly of the cross" did the vision clear for her.

"People want peace," she wrote, "but not the things that make for peace." For Dorothy, the things that "made for peace" were the daily, unstinting, unlimited works of mercy. She listed them in a 1949 article for *Commonweal* magazine and made them the centerpiece of her life. Her problem, if she had one, was that she believed in them. "The spiritual works of mercy," she recited there with all the simplicity of a school child,

are to admonish the sinner, to instruct the ignorant, to counsel the doubtful, to comfort the sorrowful, to bear wrongs patiently, to forgive all injuries, and to pray for the living and the dead. The corporal works are to feed the hungry, to give drink to the thirsty, to clothe the naked, to ransom the captive, to harbor the harborless, to visit the sick and to bury the dead.

It was a clear program and she followed it till the day she died.

She began *The Catholic Worker*, a penny newspaper, to admonish and instruct and counsel and comfort people everywhere who like her could not make sense out of a world that called itself Christian but had gone officially mad, grinding people under heel in the name of private enterprise, destroying nations in the name of liberating them, enslaving people in the name of human rights. At its peak the circulation of the paper rose to over 150,000.

She opened soup kitchens to feed the hungry and give drink to the thirsty.

She began hospitality houses to clothe the naked and harbor the harborless, to care for the sick and bury the dead. Over seventy-five groups, fundamentally independent but united in a philosophy of the Christian economics of sharing and alternative living, opened in her lifetime and more were begun even after her death.

And she ransomed those held captive to oppression and violence and technological barbarism with her very body. She is best remembered perhaps for her post-conversion opposition to U.S. participation in World War II but the fact is that her first jail sentence was for a suffragette demonstration in 1917. She spent thirty days in prison and participated in a grueling hunger strike to break the resistance of society to the demands of women. The popular opinion was that the women had won the conflict when their demands were met and they were given early release, but the experience affected

Dorothy deeply, first plunging her into depression and then firing her determination even more to do something for people everywhere who were being beaten, starved, and imprisoned to stop them from organizing against oppressive and dehumanizing conditions. The truth of the matter was that Dorothy was called to the poor long before she was called to Catholicism.

It was after her conversion to Catholicism, however, that Dorothy found the meaning she needed to go on. As a Catholic she put the scripture ahead of the system and the Gospel ahead of the government at all times in a church that itself, her communist friends were quick to point out, had long been the handmaiden of the government's theology of defense and theology of capitalism and theology of the civic religion.

In the end, Dorothy Day was herald to the church, herald to the state, and herald to the poor. And she did not do it by converting others. She did it by changing her own small corner of the world.

It is not possible to talk about Dorothy Day without talking about Peter Maurin, the French peasant with a medieval dream for a modern world, who in 1932 appeared, it seemed, out of nowhere to give Dorothy Day's restless commitment and recurring intuition a vision and a form. They were an unlikely combination, these two: Peter Maurin was raised steeped in Catholicism; Dorothy was steeped in revolutionary theory. Peter Maurin was a visionary, a theological thinker; Dorothy Day was a social activist, a writer who had been schooled in socialist ideology and the politics of protest. Together they created one of the first major truly lay movements in the history of the church, a Christian concept of economics, and the boldest peace movement of its day.

Intent simply on changing their own lives — much in the model of the great religious reformers like Benedict and Francis who had introduced whole new styles of life in the midst of their eroding worlds — Peter and Dorothy began a program of publications, conferences, and educational activities based on the social teachings of the church that ran side by side with rural communes, hospitality houses, and soup kitchens for the urban poor.

The new lifestyle attracted not only the needy themselves but hosts of young volunteers who had also heard the words of Christ burning in their hearts but seldom, if ever, had seen them realized in churches that cared for the poor but never admonished the system that made them poor or kept them poor. Dorothy herself had written in the second year of the Great Depression:

> More and more people were losing their jobs, more families were being evicted, the Unemployed Councils were being formed by the communist groups and the Workers Alliance sprang into existence. It was time for pressure groups, for direct action, and radicalism was thriving among all groups except Catholics. I felt out of it. There was Catholic membership in all these groups, of course, but no Catholic leadership. It was that very year that Pope Pius XI said sadly, "...The workers of the world are lost to the church."

Between them Peter Maurin and Dorothy Day showed the world that there was such a thing as Catholic Social Policy and that it could be lived.

To feed the hungry was one thing. To be against World War II and the nuclearization of the world was entirely another. To pursue violence as an act of justice, she taught, was un-Christian. She said without apology, "We confess to being fools [for Christ], and wish that we were more so....Dear God, please enlarge our hearts to love each other, to love our neighbor, to love our enemy as well as our friend." The state considered them subversive. The church considered them radically outside the just war tradition. People considered them seditious or traitorous or crazy. Even the circulation of the paper dropped to less than fifty thousand within a matter of months. Clearly, people who had found the works of

mercy comforting did not find love of the enemy acceptable. Charity was one thing but justice was another.

Dorothy Day persisted in her radical pacifist posture, however, warning of worse things to come if violence was met with violence, standing straight and unflinching in the heart of the church itself. At first the Catholic Worker Movement was treated at best like a misguided but basically harmless embarrassment to the institutional church. Within five years of her death, though, the Roman Catholic bishops of the United States in concert with three popes since Pius XII — John XXIII, Paul VI, and John Paul II — themselves published a pastoral on peace, condemning the arms race and allowing for conscientious objection. Popular writers had begun to talk about Roman Catholicism as "a peace church," and war resistance had become a very Catholic thing. Dorothy Day had stood firm and eventually the church had come to her. It is hard to deny the Gospel in your midst.

But approval is not what Dorothy was about. After being jailed for protesting civil defense drills in the 1950s, she wrote:

> I am not particularly interested in writing about my few days in jail last month. I am just glad that I served them, and am ready to serve again if there is another compulsory air-raid drill next summer. It is a gesture perhaps, but a necessary one. Silence means consent and we cannot consent to the militarization of our country without protest since we believe that the air-raid drills are part of a calculated plan to inspire fear of the enemy instead of the love which Jesus Christ told us we should feel toward them.

She was still going to jail at the age of seventy-five.

She was still living in a public tenement for the poor until the day she died.

She was still witnessing to a personal poverty that confronted the systemic sin of exploitation by "living simply so that others could simply live."

She was still answering the letters of people, professional Christians all, who preferred a less public display of belief, a more antiseptic religion. "If we are not being persecuted for our beliefs and life, there is something wrong with us," she wrote. Indeed, everything that people didn't like about her she ended up proving being right about. People — clergy and laity alike — didn't like her attitudes on war. Then, thirty years later, the bishops of the U.S. church wrote the first unified statement on peace. They didn't like her attitudes on capitalism. Then, thirty years later, the bishops wrote the economic pastoral. They didn't like her marching for women's voting rights. Then, seventy years later, the bishops of the church set out to begin the long, hard process of facing up to women's concerns.

The temptation, of course, is to mourn the loss of a leader in a time that cries for leadership. The difference here, however, may be that what Dorothy Day led was a revolution of attitudes and a revolution of personal responsibility. She is the icon of the kind of leader that everyone else, anyone else, can be, not by changing other people but by changing themselves.

FRANZ JAGERSTATTER
Icon of Conscience

If there is someone who would not expect to be enshrined in a volume such as this, it would certainly be Franz Jagerstatter. If there is someone in this volume whom few people know, it is probably Franz Jagerstatter.

W. H. Auden gave him brief mention in a poem once, yes, but it is rarely anthologized. The scholar and pacifist Gordon Zahn wrote a book about him. There are a few small articles and a short film. But for the most part, the man is obscure, unmarked, unknown. There are no statues in the parks of the world that freeze his posture into a noble memory. There are no ballads, no marches to retell his story. There are no flags, no banners to strut the glories of his life.

And yet, this book would be incomplete without him. In fact, this book may be more about him than about any other.

Jagerstatter was a man caught in a cruel trick of history. He was a young Austrian farmer trapped in Hitler's *anschluss* and torn between two goods — responsibility to his family and responsibility to his conscience. To this day people debate whether or not he made the right choice but, if principle is any criterion in moral decision-making at all, then the evidence is heavy in his favor.

Franz Jagerstatter chose for conscience in a climate of sin and paid for it with his life. He could have chosen for convenience, but the fact is that convenience exacts a price as well. The difference is that the price for compliance is not life lost, true. It is far worse than that: the price for compliance is life soured by the sight of our own smallness.

Franz Jagerstatter's story is the story of an ordinary man grown great under the pressures of the time.

Jagerstatter was a small farmer in a small village on the border between Austria and Germany. St. Radegund's was hardly more than a collection of small farms, and certainly not a center of intellectual stimulation or a hotbed of political ferment. On the contrary. Most of the villagers welcomed the annexation of Austria into Hitler's Third Reich. And those who did not said nothing at all. Except for Jagerstatter. In the first place, he voted against the attachment. In the second place, when others said "Heil, Hitler," Jagerstatter, the villagers recall, said "Pfui, Hitler" or, more to the point, "Gross Gott," the traditional Austrian greeting. His opposition was clear and consistent. He voted against annexation; he refused the new government's family assistance program; he declined emergency farm aid; he restrained his godson from joining the Hitler Youth Corps; he criticized the regime publicly.

But Franz Jagerstatter was not the type the world could have assumed would automatically rise to heights of serious social protest. As a young man he had been something of the village roustabout, a lusty leader of a gang of good but garrulous teenagers, the owner of the first motorcycle in the village, a hearty but somewhat undisciplined young man who had fathered an illegitimate child in the next village and been sent into temporary exile with another young man by his own townspeople in order to cool the bitterness between them before it upset the social equilibrium of the whole tightly knit area. No doubt about it: Franz Jagerstatter was no candidate for philosophical heroics.

Yet somehow, somewhere along the line, he grew into something far different from the boy next door. What had been a painfully average life became a siren of faith. What had been a normal pattern of church-going turned into searing commitment. The very fact that no one knows how the change came about, however, is perhaps the strongest argument for the normalcy of the man. There was no blinding, soul-shattering vision, apparently, no traumatic experience, no conversion moment, no life-changing event that turned Franz Jagerstatter the farmer into Franz Jagerstatter a dead but faithful fool. There was, it seems, nothing but the scripture and the liturgy, the word and the faith that took the dailiness of a basically dull life and turned it into the stuff of high holiness.

Even the "great change" villagers noted when they discussed Jagerstatter's developing religious bent was paltry in comparison to the kinds of conversion that we have come to expect at the base of great spiritual epic. There were no long fasts, no stigmata, no ecstasies, not even any displays of unusual devotion in his life. He prayed in the fields as he farmed them; he sang hymns while he worked; he went to daily Mass with the old ladies of the countryside. He was simply a young father with insights of crystal and a soul as strong as rock.

Later, the people would say that his newfound "religious fanaticism" and its end in martyrdom were due to the influence of a pious wife. His letters and her own responses to the situation simply don't confirm that explanation. If anything, it looks more like the thin rationalization of people who knew that one of their own, someone trained by the very people who had trained them, in the very concepts in which they too were trained had, in the final analysis, risen to the full implications of the spiritual life while they themselves had not.

It is so much more comforting to imagine great people as having come to greatness through a series of great events: the influence of unusual people; a dedication to unusual pious practices; the confrontation with unusual moments in history; the shock of unusual circumstances. It is so much harder to come to grips with the valor of people whose lives have been just like our own: grinding, uneventful, ordinary. It is so much harder to come to grips with our own small surrenders in life. It is so much harder to remember without twinge the times in which we ourselves did not speak out, did not stand up, did not question, did not oppose the tiny little slivers of oppression that abide in the otherwise meaningless matters of our daily lives.

For Jagerstatter, as for so many of us, there was only one defining moment in life. He recognized it. He owned it. And he met it head on. It cost him his life, yes, but the real question may well be whether his life would have been worth anything if he had not.

Jagerstatter had never approved of the Nazi regime. He had even given up going to the local inn with the other farmers of the area in order to avoid the political arguments that erupted there over the progress of the regime. It was not until August of 1943, however, that he was brought to the point of no return. Then, with World War II already almost four years old, with Germany having bogged down in Stalingrad and Rommel in full flight after the loss of Tobruk and Benghazi, with Italy's declaration of war on Germany and the commencement of Allied "round-the-clock" bombing of Germany, all the rules of the game began to collapse. Every man in the Reich who could carry a gun was subject to conscription. Franz Jagerstatter's draft notice arrived in February of 1943.

Franz Jagerstatter refused to take the military oath.

Wiser people counseled otherwise, including the parish priest, the prison chaplain, and the bishop of Linz. In every case, the advice hinged on the fact that private citizens had no responsibility to judge the actions and policies of a government; that in accepting military service he would not be endorsing Nazism but simply following orders; that he had neither the facts nor the competence to make a judgment about the justice of the war; that his primary responsibility was to his family and that the savage military policies of the Allies with their ceaseless bombing of cities and civilian populations reduced the moral implications of the service. But Jagerstatter could not be moved. Nazism was wrong; war was wrong; killing was wrong. He could not do it.

Two facets of his conviction and execution are particularly telling. In the first place, the government did relent and promise him non-combatant status. In the second place, he was in prison for six months. His decision, in other words, was not a rash act, a moment's flare, the result

of heat and temper. He had plenty of time to think it over, and he had a comparatively peaceful alternative to consider. What's more, he had a family — three young daughters and a wife — who wanted him to come home alive. In an undated farewell message, it is clear that concerns for the family weighed upon him heavily. He wrote,

> If one argues from the standpoint of the family, you need not be troubled here either; for it is not permitted to lie, even for the sake of the family. And if I had ten children, the greatest demand upon me is still the one I must make of myself.

And in another statement:

> Again and again people stress the obligations of conscience as they concern my wife and children. Yet I cannot believe that just because one has a wife and children, he is free to offend God by lying (not to mention all the other things he would be called upon to do). Did not Christ Himself say, "He who loves father, mother, or children more than Me is not deserving of My love"?

For Franz Jagerstatter, the most important thing a father had to do for his children was to be a holy man, whatever the cost. It was the ultimate life-lesson, the greatest one, the final one.

Worse yet, it was the supremely lonely one. He wrote about the role of the church in the rise of the regime:

> It is not good if our spiritual leaders remain silent year after year....Do we no longer want to see Christians who are able to take a stand in the darkness around us in deliberate clarity, calmness, and confidence — who, in the midst of tension, gloom, selfishness, and hate, stand fast in perfect peace and cheerfulness — who are not like the floating reed which is driven here and there by every breeze — who do not merely watch to see what their friends will do but instead ask themselves, "What does our faith teach us about this," or "can my conscience bear this so easily that I will never have to repent?"

But Jagerstatter had no one at all on his side, no one to tell him of the purity of his act or the sensibilities of his soul. He had nothing to rely on at all except his conscience, a conscience raw as winter wind and sharp as honed steel, the conscience of a simple farmer who had been raised on the most fundamental of truths:

In the "Statement of Position" he wrote his lawyer to explain his refusal to take the military oath, he asserts:

> The true Christian is to be recognized more in works and deed than in speech. The surest mark of all is found in deeds showing love of neighbor. To do unto one's neighbor what one would desire for oneself is more than merely not doing to others what one would not want done to oneself. Let us love our enemies, bless those who curse us, pray for those who persecute us. For love will conquer and will endure for all eternity. And happy are they who live and die in God's love.

They executed Franz Jagerstatter with hardly a notice. Who would remark the loss of one more farmer, one more soldier, one more anguished soul in the world's greatest military massacre of all time? As he himself had explained to his wife, taking the military oath would not guarantee his life. Those who refused to fight for an unjust regime in an unjust war died, true, but those who fought died in the soul as well as in the body.

Death was of the essence of Nazi Germany, and in a culture of death no one notices who has died or how. Death was the nature of the place.

This death, in particular, seemed at first to be unbearably futile. It started no revolution, ended no conflict, eliminated no evil. But years later, they began to come to St. Radegund's one at a time, people looking for proof that the personal is possible even in the face of the powerful and oppressive. At the time it did nothing, this death, but it seeded a peace movement twenty-five years later. It did absolutely nothing — then — but it cast such a single, strong, solitary shadow of resistance against evil that it gives substance to conscience everywhere years later. It did nothing then, but it is clear sign now that no single act is meaningless.

Franz Jagerstatter is an icon of the single-mindedness of God. Perhaps that is the very purpose of life, to spend one's years in preparation for just such a moment when all the soul of life becomes focused in one act. It is true, of course, that most of us might never have to make such a choice, but, oh, to be ready might be worth the life.

KATERI TEKAKWITHA
Icon of Otherness

The interesting thing about time is that though it tends, on the one hand, to minimize people as the long view of history dissolves what was once considered heroic into an indistinct stream, on the other hand, it tends to embellish and crystallize and magnify some of them as well. We come to know, at least, that they were great for their day. What is often more difficult is to realize that they may be just as great for our own. The reason for the confusion lies not so much, it seems, in the quality of the person themselves as it does in the meaning that each period is able to give to them. Kateri Tekakwitha is surely such a figure.

Kateri Tekakwitha has been defined to represent everything that now embarrasses us about an earlier age. She was an Indian who was considered valuable only because she became a Christian. She was a woman who chose the "higher life" of virginity. She was a pietist who punished her body with great penances. Or, to put it another way: she was valued, it seems, because she gave up Indian ways for the ways of the whites and so denied what she was, because she gave up a natural life in favor of a "supernatural" one, because she brutalized the body in favor of the soul.

The question is, are those really the qualities that make Kateri Tekakwitha a model for all of us now?

The answer is, look at Kateri Tekakwitha again.

The answer is not an easy one. The situation is a great deal more complex than it would seem.

Kateri Tekakwitha was born in 1656 in a village called Ossernenon on the Mohawk River. It was not a propitious time in Indian history. In the first place, French trappers had made incursions on Indian territory, diminishing their lands and threatening their livelihood. In the second place, the great Indian nations of the Iroquois and Algonquins were themselves at war over control of the fur trade with the French. It was a clash of strong and clearly defined cultures.

The Algonquins were a proud people, the most numerous of American Indians north of the Rio Grande and the most widespread. They were also the most foreign to white ways. They were roving hunters, nomads who went from hunting ground to hunting ground, traveling light, uninterested in amassing things, loving the months they hunted and loving the months they didn't, turning indigence into virtue.

The stability of the Algonquin did not come from land; it came from tradition. A sense of creation, a contemplative sense of the Great Spirit who permeated the earth, a sense of conservatism guided everything they did. And custom was its glue. There was a way to do everything. And

ἩΑΓΙΑ ᾽ΑΙΚΑΤΕΡΙΝΑ

KATERI TEKAKWITHA of the IROQUOIS

though whites often missed the truth of it and called them savages and dismissed them out of hand for their lack of self-control, their slavery to their natural impulses, the truth of the matter was just the opposite. For the Algonquin, there was a very strict discipline to be honed. There were charges to be laid at the feet of those who broke the tribal laws, the most effective of which was ridicule. It was laughter that the Algonquin feared most, the kind of laughter that comes with scorn. It was public disdain, not physical punishment, that most assured the keeping of Algonquin customs.

They were as well a passive people who had learned to wait. They were stoics who suffered in silence.

Kateri Tekakwitha's mother was a disciplined and contemplative Algonquin. She had been taken captive in an intertribal war and saved by the Mohawk chief of the Iroquois nation to whom she was then married. Kateri Tekakwitha's father, therefore, was an Iroquois. From the Iroquois strain, Kateri inherited a world view entirely other than the Algonquin.

The Iroquois, unlike the Algonquin, were a group of smaller tribes whose strength lay in the fact that they had united. The League of Nations established by the Iroquois gave them peace among the five nations — the Mohawks, the Oneidas, the Onondagas, the Cayugas, and the Senecas — and strength in the Indian world despite their smaller numbers.

At the same time, the Iroquois were known for their cruelty. They had raised torture to high art, a skill they had learned in their contact with the Aztec culture and its history of human sacrifice. Torture for them was a religious ritual, designed to give glory to the god of war and therefore done slowly, done well. Isaac Jogues, observers testified, had his skin stripped from him and eaten on the way back to the village where he was finally, after days of worse torture, mercifully executed.

Pain in general, in fact, held high place in Iroquois culture. Even children competed with one another in their ability to bear suffering. Missionaries recounted hearing small children sing songs of joy when kettles of boiling hot water were spilled on them, without a cry, without a tear. Pain was not something designed merely for others by these people. Nor was pain a physical exercise, a preparation for war, a manifestation of male endurance. To the Iroquois, pain was a sacrifice that made people greater than they would normally be. They were, in other words, a highly ascetic people.

The Iroquois were also a highly communal people, an agricultural people, whose long houses held as many as fifty people or five families each, in contrast to the Algonquin, who lived in private, single-family huts that were easily broken down and easily reassembled as they traveled from season to season back and forth across the land in search of better hunting grounds.

In Iroquois culture, too, women counted. Descent was marked through women. It was men who moved into the bride's long house rather than she into his in order to keep a man from marrying a blood sister. It was women who were in charge of the fields, the most important possession of the tribe. Women, in other words, stood for the perpetuity that the Iroquois valued so highly. Women were the guardians of the ceremonies. Women were the keepers of the peace who had the right to save or to condemn the prisoners of the tribe. Women were a factor to be reckoned with in the matter of values and judgment and the preservation of the clan.

Most of all, the Iroquois respected their ancestors and cared for their dead. Every ten years, for reasons of public health and care for the land, the Iroquois changed their village site. And every ten years, they disinterred the bones of their dead and carried them with them. The ancestors, the past, lived in their bones. The cult of the dead gave them strength of soul. They were never alone; they were never without guidance; they were never without purpose as long as they walked in the way of their ancestors.

But the cult of the dead also oppressed them. The Iroquois owed a debt to the past that they paid every day of their lives. What had been given to them by their ancestors they were required to retain for the future. When the Five Nations met for condolence ceremonies, they sang of the communal debt:

I come again to greet and thank the League;
I come again to greet and thank the kindred;
I come again to greet and thank the warriors;
I come again to greet and thank the women.
My forebears—what they established—
My forebears—hearken to them.

And hearken she did. Kateri Tekakwitha was a fair blend of both traditions, prayerful and contemplative like the Algonquin, strong and stoic and able to bear pain like the Iroquois. The two qualities translated into a Christian life that captivated the Indians and astonished the French Jesuits who were her directors.

Kateri was an Indian living in the midst of a demoralized people. Orphaned at the age of four by a smallpox epidemic that spared her life but scarred her face and weakened her eyes, Kateri was raised by her father's brother as his own. Her mother had been Christian, but she herself had not been baptized, and, frankly, Kateri showed very little interest until, by terms of the latest peace treaty, a Jesuit came to live among them. Then the contrast between the values of Christianity and the degree of drunkenness and depravity emerging around her were stark and clear. Then the prayerful Algonquin, the strong Mohawk woman in her wanted more out of life than indigence and moral deterioration. A missionary at the village, Father Bruyas, describes in his diary what the drunkenness among the Indians was like. Spawned by French fur-traders to enable the companies to trade cheap brandy for expensive beaver skins, it destroyed the moral fiber of whole tribes. For a time the

excommunication by Bishop Laval against those who sold liquor to Indians was the only sanction against its unregulated distribution. Father Bruyas wrote:

The 16th. People return from trading, with sixty kegs of brandy brought from new Holland. A drunken man breaks in the door of my Chapel, reproaching me for the insolence of our Frenchmen. Another strikes my companion, with such violence that he bears the mark of it. Owing to the disorders that are prevailing in this Village, I take occasion to go on a trip toward our Lake, where there are some fishermen—although I am still very weak from a tertian fever.... The heaviest cross that I have is that of the drunkards; and I have need of all my little virtue to bear it patiently. It breaks up all our exercises, and all our teaching; and prevents the people from coming to the Chapel to say their prayers, morning and evening—each one thinking only of running away and hiding, in order to avoid the violence of these furious men.

It was an environment like that from which Kateri escaped to join a settlement begun by the Jesuits to isolate baptized Indians from the influence of their tribes. The conclusion both of history and of a new theology of mission is that villages like this one de-Indianized the Indians, denigrated their culture, and denied the very basis for real evangelization and destroyed any hope of true inculturation of the faith. For the simple purpose of spotlighting Christianity, however, the missionaries of the time instituted few more effective projects than these Christian mission towns where Indians left their own tribes to live another kind of life.

The important thing about Kateri Tekakwitha, however, is that her stay in the Jesuit village of Caughnawaga cast a beacon both ways. She was not only a sign to the Indians; she was also a sign to the whites that is valid and valuable to this day.

Kateri Tekakwitha had three outstanding qualities that reflected and challenged both the period and the place: First, she was extremely pious. Second, she was a dedicated virgin. Third, she was devoted to the theology of the cross and to the meaning of human suffering in life. Each of those qualities was a sign of contradiction to Indians and whites alike. Each of them has something to say to the present age as well.

The Indians, dissipated and demoralized in the face of the superior power of the white nations, the loss of power, and the encroachment on their territories, found her piety an annoying challenge to their own loss of spirit and a disturbing call to conversion of character, either Christian or tribal. This Algonquin woman, contemplative from her roots, was a reminder of higher things and lasting values and the demands of the spirit among a people on the verge of losing them. They made fun of her. They ridiculed her. They scorned her. And she persisted to the point of their respect.

But she was just as much a sign of contradiction to the whites. The policy at the mission was that Indians, baptized or not, were not permitted to receive the Eucharist earlier than two years after their conversion. These were, after all, "barbarians," "savages." What's more, frequent Communion, so common in contemporary society, whose theology teaches that communion is a support, a grace rather than a reward for the perfect, was rare for anyone in Jansenist France. Worse than that, the wartime practices of the Iroquois were seen as half-cannibal. Who knows what they were thinking about receiving "the body and blood of Christ"? Finally, the highest synods of the Western world were submitting to serious debate about whether or not Indians really had souls, whether or not Indians were fit matter for ordination, whether or not Indians were fully human. In this theological environment, Kateri Tekakwitha was a shining sign not just of humanity, of soul, of chosenness, but of holiness. Sanctity. Communion with God. She was a sobering rebuttal to the thinking of white, Western theologians. After all,

if the Indian was only half-souled, how could they possibly be saintly? But she was. And by their own standards.

Kateri's virginity, her firm refusal to marry, and her commitment to live a nun-like life despite the fact that a white church did not accept native Indians as nuns was a sign to the Indian population that the marriage laws of the white world could be followed and its Christian commitment to them was possible. To the whites, her virginity was a manifestation of a woman's strength to commit herself entirely to God in the face of all odds and pressures, without institutional support, without cloister, without public restraint, and without a habit. It was a stinging rebuke to a church in which its archtheologian Thomas Aquinas had taught that women did not have "sufficient strength of mind to resist concupiscence" and which at that very time was refusing to let white nuns operate in public places without rigid controls.

Finally, Kateri, good Iroquois that she was, bore suffering heroically. To the Indians she was, therefore, a symbol of how great a human being could be. To the whites, her commitment to penance was a sign of discipline in a culture they viewed as completely without human and rational control.

Booker T. Washington wrote once: "You measure the size of the accomplishment by the obstacles you had to overcome to reach your goals." What may look like standard-brand Christian accomplishments to us today were, in Kateri's time, obstacles of measure on both sides. More than that, however, in a period of racism and sexism and national domination, Kateri Tekakwitha needs to be discovered again. She is a sign of God's presence in non-whites. She is a call to the conversion of whites. She was a sign of contradiction to two cultures and a prophetic presence in both. She is an icon of otherness.

TERESA of AVILA
Face of Fire

To be a woman is not easy in any period of history. The world is a male preserve, and women, it has apparently been decreed by someone, somewhere for his own convenience, are to be its caretakers, not its pioneers. To be a strong and idealistic woman is even worse. The problem is that caretaking is not usually the gift of dreamers who have an urge to change things, but if the dreamers are women, it is even worse. Leadership is normally denied a woman under the best of circumstances, and only caretaking is acceptable. The result is a kind of human in-betweenness for women that confuses the psyche and lacerates the soul. It is a state of life that has plagued most of the great women of the world. As a result, women have commonly been fated to live undeveloped lives, to live vicariously, to find their fulfillment and satisfaction in life in the lives of their husbands and children or else be doomed to find little if any satisfaction at all.

Teresa of Avila was that kind of woman — too bright for her time, too strong for the institutions around her, too spiritual for the church of her day. To be a woman in a society that does not value women as full human beings brings with it the burden of invisibility. To be a woman with different views about the ideals of life brings with it the burden of ostracism. To be a woman with an independent interior life too often brings with it the suspicions of what in life was most dear to her, the church. Teresa of Avila had all three problems: she was a strong woman in a male culture; she was an institutional reformer in a period of high satisfaction; she was a visionary in a time of orthodoxy. It was a difficult, a dynamic mix.

The social situation in sixteenth-century Spain was a vibrant but oppressive one. In the first place, Spain was fresh from two of the highest achievements of its history. Spain had just expelled the Moslems from the south and with them the threat of Islam as a European power. At the same time, Spain's discovery of the New World had made the country a symbol of prestige, a new base of European power and a vein of wealth. While social change and philosophical tension rocked the rest of Europe, Spain basked in its newfound security and sense of self. Spain, Catholic Spain, was very much at ease with itself. After all, Spain had saved the West by vanquishing the infidel and, it seemed, saved the church as well perhaps by opening up a new world to conversion when the old one was rocked by protest. No doubt about it: to be Spanish and Catholic was to delight in both nationalism and religious fidelity, one concept not to be divorced from the other.

The continent, on the other hand, was a hotbed of tension and turmoil, of ideas in flux and institutions in confusion.

Between the years 1500 and 1545, Erasmus, the most influential of the Christian humanists, was satirizing the corruptions of the clergy. The burning of books that attacked the authority of the church had been ordered by papal decree. Humanism was emphasizing the central importance of human values as opposed to religious beliefs. The Protestant reformers were speaking out. Martin Luther rebelled against the church's selling of indulgences. England dissolved 376 religious houses. The Inquisition was approved by Pope Paul III in 1542. One year later, the Index of Forbidden Books was published and the first victims of the Spanish Inquisition were burned at the stake. Peasant groups were revolting all across Europe, Machiavelli was writing

about how to maintain political control, and the church had opened the Council of Trent in 1545 to counteract the effects of Protestantism. New religious groups — the Oratorians, the Jesuits, the Capuchins — were rising to spearhead the reforms spiritually. It was a period of new ideas, new repressions, and new problems.

Teresa de Ahumada, later to be better known as Teresa of Avila, found herself in the midst of all of them. She was a woman, a Spaniard, a religious. In those days, any one of those categories would have been defining. To be a woman limited a person to a life of frills and superficiality. To be a Spaniard in a time of global discovery gave new scope and energy and vision. To be a religious marked a person for a kind of pious parasitism.

Teresa of Avila, born in 1515, entered a convent in 1536, just at the point when Spain was feeling most fattened with its achievements, both economic and religious. The feeling permeated everything. At the Convent of the Incarnation, for instance, if religious life was not totally corrupt, it was at least mediocre, satisfied, and largely without life-changing purpose, more soporific than challenge to the human soul.

The dilemma is that the worst thing that can happen to religious life is not difficulty. The worst thing that can happen to religious life is security, satisfaction, and approval. In newly united Spain, Catholicism was a social status, not a social conscience. By the time the unusually beautiful twenty-one-year-old Teresa de Ahumada entered the Carmelite Convent of the Incarnation to do penance for her sins — a response to her mother's early death and the questionable state of her own health — religious life had settled into the most conventional, most social of religious enclaves. Fearing an early death herself, she embarked on the ascetic life to prepare for it. But serious asceticism was not what Spanish convents were about in those days. Spanish Carmels were long past their first fervor and, in the climate of the times, had gone spiritually dry. They had become, for the most part, places of routine that

Ἡ ἁγία ΘΕΡΕCΙΑ ἡ τȣ Ἰησȣ

ST. TERESA OF AVILA

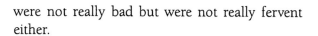

were not really bad but were not really fervent either.

Though the dowry provided by Teresa's father entitled her to private rooms and higher status, the convent itself was not fully endowed. The nuns made their living by taking *devotos,* or advisees, many of them wealthy young men with the leisure and the resources to purchase that kind of spiritual attention. The problem was that those who came repeatedly to the large, unsupervised convent for direction ran the danger of becoming more of a pastime than a focus for service and ministry. Worse, the situation was a seedbed for ardent liaisons, some spiritual, but not all of them. More than that, the internal discipline of the convent itself was weak. The nuns went for long visits to secular friends and families at will. Work was almost non-existent. Instead of concentrating a person on the spiritual life, the convent regime was itself a challenge to it. Teresa herself—personable, charming, perfumed, vivacious, and attractive to men her entire life—wrote later about the urbanity, the triviality of the situation. The dichotomy between what she said she was and what she was really doing with her life, in fact, caused Teresa great tension and, some say, may well have led to the physical breakdown that changed her life.

Whatever the origin of the illness that paralyzed her for almost three years, her autobiographical account of this period talks at length about the young men "who troubled her soul" and the guilt she felt at living a double life. After this illness, Teresa didn't simply re-enter the convent. She re-entered the community with an eye to changing first herself and then, eventually, to changing religious life itself.

The motivation seems standard and the scenarios almost mythical: a great sinner becomes sick and then becomes a great saint whom people follow with adoring hearts and perfect trust. For Teresa, though the change was real, it was not immediate and it was definitely not welcomed, by her or almost anybody else. For years she went

on struggling between her love of the salon-like atmosphere of the Convent of the Incarnation and the underlying search for something more, something deeper. She wrote later of this period:

> It is one of the most painful lives, I think, that one can imagine; for neither did I enjoy God nor did I find happiness in the world. When I was experiencing the enjoyments of the world, I felt sorrow when I recalled what I owed to God. When I was with God, my attachments to the world disturbed me. This is a war so troublesome that I don't know how I was able to suffer it even a month, much less for so many years.

It took twenty years, in fact, before the spiritual life that developed during her illness impelled the changes that became the reform of the order and through the order the spirituality of the society around it. In those years, Teresa developed the prayer life that would become both her virtue and her scourge, her strength and the basis for the suspicions in which she was held. Her prayer, in the spirit of the Christian humanism of Erasmus and its search for direct experiences of God, became "personal." She began to talk about the voice of God directing her in a period when false mystics were being tried—and burned—for witchcraft. Worst of all, she wanted to reinstate the Primitive Rule of the order and introduce a whole new kind of prayer life—her own—into a community that was quite comfortable the way it was.

Teresa of Avila faced what anybody faces who sets out to make a system work or a business ethical or a country moral. She was opposed at every level by the people from whom she should have been able to expect the most support: from the nuns themselves, the ranking members of the order, and from the officials of both church and state. Finally, she was plagued by self-doubt.

In the first place, Teresa took twenty years to begin her reform with serious intent, which means that she herself had been no model of higher aspirations. For twenty years after her recovery, she fluctuated between her attempts to develop a deep and meaningful personal prayer life and the continual diversions of the convent. She says later about the period that she found then "neither any joy in God nor any pleasure in the world." On the other hand, by the time she began to consider the founding of her first Reformed Convent at the age of forty-five, there was no doubt that she knew both what she did want and what she did not. She wanted what her prayer-life demanded: a commitment that was simple, regular, and stripped of aimless temporizing between what was prompted by sacred ideals and what was dictated by secular tastes. She wanted what she heard the Voice of God directing her to do.

Needless to say, her ideas were anything but popular with the rest of the nuns at the Convent of the Incarnation, good women surely but not the intensely religious kind, who had accepted the social definition of religious life with hardly a passing moment of wonder.

The officials of the order labeled the plan "proud" and grounded in a false sense of call and revelation and wanted no part of the uproar that it had started.

The public had all the convents it felt it could afford and, fearing that groups without clear means of support would simply become burdens to society, rioted at the very thought of opening another one — and this one sworn to the most rigorous type of poverty.

Teresa found herself on fire with a new vision of religious life and very much alone with it.

Finally, the church itself was the greatest obstacle to reform. The church, in fact, had had all the reformers it intended to abide. A woman claiming a special relationship with God was particularly unwelcome. Old women with liver spots on their hands were considered marked by the devil and were being burned all over Europe. Lonely old widows with pets were condemned for having had intercourse with the devil in the form of

their cats. Old women who were the herbalists of the century were accused of knowing demonic potions. The *Malleus Mallificarum*, The Hammer of Sorceresses, published in 1486 in Germany and given imprimatur by the officials of the church, was growing in popularity. In Spain itself, although only twelve witches were burned at the stake, five thousand were put on trial. The threat of danger for those who saw church and God and prayer differently from the church of Rome was real. The church was preserving itself by stamping out its opposition.

Ironically enough, Teresa of Avila was the opposition. She fostered a form of prayer new to church circles. Called "mental prayer," it departed from the formulas of the official Latin prayers and was, therefore, suspect for heresy and hysteria. She was promoting a new prayer style that was undefined, uncontrolled. It abandoned the Latin prayer forms of the church in a Tridentine period when formulas on every level were becoming more and more defined as the only answer to the loss of church control and the personal interpretations of Protestant reformers. For a long time, as a result, Teresa of Avila herself was a subject for Inquisitors. In the first place, her prayer was too personal and so, they declared, too Protestant; in the second place, she was hardly anti-Semitic enough since her father himself was Jewish; in the third place, she was starting something new.

Inquisition was an age-old convention. Roman emperors instituted the use of force against heretics for the simple reason that the identification of the church with the state made heresy in one treason in the other. Inquisitors were entrusted with powers independent of the local episcopal authority. Their methods, zealous and well-intentioned perhaps, were at the same time brutal and weighted in favor of the accuser. Victims were accused on the basis of anonymous complaints. They were not allowed witnesses in their favor nor were they given legal support. Confessions were gained through a standard of torture precisely prescribed in the bull of Innocent IV of 1252, *Ad Extirpanda*. The goal was the preservation of church authority. Justice and truth, individuality and private piety were too often the victims of the process. Good connections at court, King Ferdinand himself in fact, gave Teresa support and special privilege in the process. One biographer writes that the defense of her book by a theologian of the period "also defended her." While her book, he argues, says "too much about visions, which are always to be mistrusted, and especially in women," it is clear that "while she may be deceived she is at least no deceiver," for one less honest "would not have told the facts of her life so plainly…both the evil and the good." Educated men, he went on to explain, would find it of help in understanding women's confessions. The Inquisition, however, impounded her spiritual autobiography, even in the face of the arguments of "educated men."

But Teresa went on, her crisp voice and clear language calling the simplest of people to the heights of the spiritual life. "You must know that there is a time for partridge and a time for penance," she said. She criss-crossed Spain in a dangerous and difficult time, fanning fervor and founding communities committed to living Carmelite life in a new spirit. "Strive like the strong until you die in the attempt," she wrote, "for you are here for nothing else than to strive." She trusted the spirit of God in herself as much as she trusted anyone around her. "The Creator must be sought through the creatures," she taught. She went on developing a process of "mental prayer" that revolutionized religious life from a series of exercises to a way of life lived in God. "In every little thing created by God there is more than we realize, even in so small a thing as a tiny ant," she said.

"There is no happiness that is secure and nothing that does not change.…If only we thought carefully about the things of life, we should each find by experience how little either of happiness or of unhappiness there is to be got from it," she believed and set about creating a religious life that did not depend on present comforts for its quality and character. In her communities, no class distinctions were permitted to exist. Every nun participated in the physical labors of the community, despite their social rank or the size of their dowries. They wore coarse clothes and hemp sandals to underscore their commitment to poverty and things sacred rather than mundane. And they concentrated always on developing a prayer life that made the presence of God more reality than magic, more intimacy with the divine than discipline of the body.

Teresa of Avila was, by her own admission, a sinner who never doubted the mercy of God. She was a very human human being who became a saint without becoming a plastic personality, a visionary who never surrendered her vision to the politics or pressures of life.

Teresa of Avila is an icon of humanity, of vibrancy, of fire and of hope in any world bent on bending the spirit of a new age to the shape of the past. She is a sign that perseverance can cut through reaction and persistence can overcome resistance. She is clear and resounding sign that a woman can hear the word of God and do it, all male institutions to the contrary. She is a call to a spiritual life that is more impelled by vision than secure in its complacency. She taught generation after generation how to pray themselves into the presence of God, and she never used prayer as an excuse to run away from life. She wrote: "What is the purpose of prayer, my sisters? The purpose of prayer is always good works, good works, good works." And given her unending attempts to make religion spiritual and the church holy, God knows, she of all people has the right to say so.

AMOS
The Icon of Compassion

Prophets are a motley sort who bear little resemblance to one another except that all of them have a sense of what's missing in life and are committed to saying so. They come from every walk in life and every social level. For years they seem harmless enough, normal people in normal situations, until suddenly they get an insight into life that will not go away. Then there is no stopping them.

The problem is that they do not always communicate their newly found understandings with finesse and polish. In fact, what is more likely the case, they often make their announcements entirely without nuance or political adroitness. Prophets, in other words, are not always the world's smoothest people nor are they, as a result, its most popular. They talk about things that hurt. They talk about what people are not supposed to talk about at all. And they talk about it unceasingly.

Amos was perhaps the farthest out of line of them all. Amos, a person of some substance it seems as a shepherd or sheep-owner from the southern kingdom of Israel, felt impelled by God

to make a social critique of a society that was more than satisfied with itself. Amos prophesied to a world that was totally complacent. In the time of Amos Israel was at its most powerful and prosperous peak since the time of David. Its boundaries had been extended to an unprecedented degree. As far as the merchants and the military and the monarch were concerned, Yahweh was blessing Israel. Amos, in other words, was totally out of step with his times.

Amos had the effrontery to question how power and prosperity had come to Israel. Amos cited war crimes and tax foreclosures and "failures at the gate," where the elders met for the purpose of meting out justice but decided routinely against the poor, while, all the time, worship went on regularly at the shrines. "Do not seek out Bethel ... Do not go to Gilgal ... Do not journey to Beersheba," Amos warned the pilgrims and the pious. "Instead, let justice reign at the city gate!" But no one listened.

Their theology told them that they were special to God. Their worship told them that they were good since its frequency alone lulled them into thinking that their relationship with God was intact. Their wealth told them that their thick, rich, comfortable lifestyles were actually the sign of God's beneficence to them.

Indeed, the book of Amos reads like yesterday's newspaper: Yahweh is baffled, the scripture says, that the very people who had themselves been brought out of slavery in Egypt were now the oppressors of others. They were waging war. They were turning farm families into exiles. They were corrupting justice by taxing the wheat of the small farmers and turning away the needy. They were living off the backs of the poor.

Amos, impelled by the will of Yahweh, saw the situation in a burst of holy awareness and begged the powerful to recommit themselves to the vision of God. More than that, he preached that formalism in religion was worse than useless.

The message of Amos is a very strong one to people who think they are already holy. Amos tells us, in essence, to forget the amount of money we put in collection baskets, to quit presenting as credentials the number of early Masses we attend; to stop trying to kid ourselves by the size of our building donations. God, Amos says, wants much more than that. God wants our lives. God wants a new point of view from us. God wants us to want the will of God more than we want our own comfort and consolation. God wants us to pay attention to the poor. "Let justice flow like water," the scripture reads. Give more than the minimum. Give everyone their human due. Give everyone God's will for them.

And so, then and there, Amos is called to give up his nice private life as an owner of sheep in the pure and open desert and gets sent into the city to remind us all what religion is really meant to be about.

But the establishment – the high priest of Bethel itself – ran Amos out of town: "We want no more prophesying in Bethel; this is the national temple."

Anyone who has dared to question modern society with its ill-gotten oil and high-tech military and runaway economic system knows the scenario. The world does not want a prophetic religion; the world wants the type of religion that makes life comfortable. The system wants a religion of private consolation rather than a religion based on the kind of public commitment that brings inequity into question.

And there, for any novice to see, are all the contradictions and all the ironies of what it still means for anyone to be called by God. In the first place, Amos is a strange, unlikely messenger. Shepherding is nice work but hardly the stuff of which public influence is made, then or now. Secondly, the priest is a strange adversary. If no one else can, surely the priest would be able to recognize the voice of God. Then, too, this rich country is pitiably poor for all its wealth. They have money but they do not have values. And, finally, the people to whom Amos is trying to speak don't want to hear bad news when things are going fine for the privileged of them.

The parallels are all too clear. To be a religious person in today's world too is to claim commitment in a society that taxes the poor more than it does the rich. Like Israel, we too wage war on the innocent in the deserts of undeveloped nations and profit handsomely from it. We too terrorize whole peoples into exile for the sake of national political advantage. We too turn away the needy at the city gates of the richest country in the world in the name of job security while the industries of this country gain unconscionable profits from the unjust wages of Third World laborers.

Like Amos, we too are the ones being asked now to listen to the voice of God in our own lives, to leave what we were doing and to stand for something other than what this world takes for granted. We are the ones now who are expected to speak for the poor and the forgotten of our world. We are the ones being asked to do justice rather than to fool ourselves with the kind of pious niceties of religion that are just as likely to keep us from God as they are to take us there if all they do is to chloroform us to the lack of God's will in the world.

From Amos, then, we must learn first to hear the word of God ourselves so that we can tell the voice of God from all the other voices that are clamoring for attention all around us: the voice of money; the voice of career; the voice of comfort; the voice of independence; the voice of status; the voice of a world gone deaf with lesser messages than the will of God.

Like Amos we have to make a new decision every day about whether or not we are willing to be called from our own good works — as Amos was — from being good professionals and responsible civil servants and devoted workers to do an even better work as witness to the just and loving mind of God. Shepherding flocks, after all, is honorable, steady employment to this day. But it was not enough for Amos. Amos was being called out of his good, private life, with all of its value, to live a life planted in the mind of God for the sake of others. Amos was being called to be an icon of the just and compassionate face of God.

ἉΓΊΑ ΜΑΡΊΑ

PRAY FOR THE DEAD AND FIGHT LIKE HELL FOR THE LIVING!

MOTHER JONES OF AMERICA

MOTHER JONES
God's Righteous Anger

According to the proverb's teaching, "there is a point at which forbearance ceases to be a virtue." "If we had been better people we would have been angrier oftener," the essayist Bentley wrote. In a period of wanton oppression, holy anger is a virtue that the world craves. Mother Jones is its icon.

Mary Jones was born in Cork, Ireland, in 1830. She worked as a seamstress and schoolteacher, bore four children, emigrated to the United States when Victorianism was in its heyday, and, at an early age, lost both her husband and all her children to smallpox. She was one of thousands of strong and long-suffering women who lived in poverty and survived it. She bore the sins of the country on her back and was not broken by them. When workers were not paid, not protected, not secure in their back-breaking jobs, Mother Jones suffered through it all and managed to perdure. In her long, black dress and broad-brimmed hat, she was the prototype of every turn-of-the-century grandmother in the United States. Except that she wasn't. Underneath the patina of propriety and modest seemliness beat the heart of the lion of Judah who knew injustice and decried it, who knew the story of Exodus and believed it.

She was a struggling contemporary of Andrew Carnegie and John D. Rockefeller. She lived during the period of the rise of the railroads, the invention of the telegraph, the production of automatic revolvers, the passage of the U.S. Gag Law. The law was aimed at suppressing the growing debate on slavery and the specter of day labor, the practice of hiring people by the day or sometimes only by the hour at slave wages to do temporary tasks rather than to afford a process of production that would provide steady work to sustain the laboring class. Immigrant laborers especially were prey to a system that made great wealth for the monopolies, the trusts, and the financiers at the expense of the poor. "The Gilded Age" they called it, the age in which things looked beautiful on the surface—looked like progress and development and abundance — but which, underneath, were balanced on a seething, rusting mountain of the powerless. The seventy-two-hour work week, the exploitation of child labor, the sweat shops, the slum housing projects, the lockout of laborers who protested the inhuman working conditions, the blacklisting or universal rejection of laborers who dared to complain, a court system for industry rather than the work force that produced the products—all these gave painful birth to the U.S. labor movement. And Mary Harris Jones was in the midst of it. After the death of her family, Mary Jones was forced to support herself as a seamstress again by making clothes for the rich. From this very distinct vantage point she saw in a special way the plight of the poor who were at the mercy of the controlling corporate class. Wages were what employers were willing to pay, not what the value of the work could justly demand. For the average laborer, every day was an uncertain one. The future depended on how many years a person was able to work. It depended more on how often work was able to be snatched away from other hungry workers who were younger perhaps or more agile or stronger-looking as they stood in the long lines of laborers who waited like thin, emaciated birds outside bleak, unwelcoming factories for a ration of life. To be part of the labor force was to wait for owners to toss the *hoi polloi* a few crumbs, if and when there were crumbs left to toss.

The day-laborer Mary Jones became a founding member of the Knights of Labor, a utopian organization that welcomed blacks, immigrants, and women into its ranks but that, having turned violent in the Haymarket Square Incident, lost public credibility and effectiveness. But Mary Harris was not discouraged. Committed to the God-given quality of the task, she waded into mining towns to establish the United Mine Workers. She organized "mop and broom brigades" of the miners' wives who beat on pans to scare the mules away from hauling coal from the mines and so disturb production. She organized a "Children's Strike" around the motto "We want time to play." She became an all-round holy gadfly.

The miners called the staunch old lady "Mother Jones," a title she valued far more than "Madam."

With a kind of prophetic passion, she spent sixty years of her life organizing for the labor union movement and compared it to the flight of the Jews from Egypt. What Moses did, she figured, was simply to organize the Jews to confront their Egyptian slave masters. And she set about to do the same. She routed the industrial giants who dragged her off to jails and away from one industrial site after another by refusing to quit, whatever the abuse they meted out, and by refusing to keep silent, whatever the cost. "Fight like hell till you get to heaven," she counseled people,

and she gave them fair idea of how it was to be done as well.

Mother Jones was seventy-two years old when a federal representative called her "the most dangerous woman in America." She burned all her life with the fire of justice, and singed everyone she touched with it.

She was an unlikely Moses in an unlikely desert, and we have need of the likes of Mother Jones again. We need ordinary people like Mary Harris Jones, uncommonly common folk, clerks and waitresses, lathe operators and stewardesses, nurses and assembly line workers, who refuse to accept the fact that the government has money to burn on missiles it does not need but has not a penny to spend on milk for babies or higher education for the poor or an updated infrastructure for a nation. "Big government" they call it when it is designed to provide programs for average people. "Investment incentives" they call it when it is designed to provide unconscionable profits for the rich. "Repatriation of profits" they call it when it is designed to exploit the cheap labor of Third World countries with never a cent of taxes paid to the people for development of their own country in return. Indeed, Mother Jones needs to rise again in all of us.

The problem is, of course, that we so easily abstract ourselves from the ranks of the heroic and the brave. They constitute, we assume, a species beyond dailiness, beyond the neighborhood, beyond the realms of the normal. We admire them and we sometimes even follow them, but we seldom, if ever, see them in the mirror of our lives. And that's where Mother Jones comes in: old, female, grandmotherly, widowed, childless, and financially destitute, she is the phantom of all our powerless lives. The difference between Mother Jones and most of the rest of humankind is that Mother Jones looked at the world through the eyes of God and announced what she saw: exploitation, corruption, and injustice. Then, piece by little piece, she did something to change it: a mining town here, a meeting there.

What was, was not enough for her. And thanks to her, a rich and massive system was forced to change.

"Where is your home?" they asked her. "I abide where there is any fight against wrong," she answered them. "My address is like my shoes — it travels with me."

The icon is a clear one.

Mother Jones is a model of perseverance. By the time she died at the age of one hundred she had spent the greater part of her life speaking out for the needs of others, for the reform of a system engineered to misuse the weak and engorge the strong. She wanted to win her battle against the owners of the production system but losing didn't stop her. Success was not nearly as important to her as truth. What was right was right and she was wedded to it all her adult life. No gain was enough to justify calling the battle won when there was more to do. No achievement made the next move unnecessary. No amount of concessions bought her off the trail of the dishonesty that remained to be exposed.

Mother Jones — soft, old, female — gave early warning of the power of powerlessness to all the robber barons of the world. There was simply no way to withstand the onslaught of truth that would not be stilled. She stands as sign to this day of what people can do in a world that feigns deafness to truth if only they decide to shout it without ceasing.

Mother Jones is an antidote to ageism in a society that glorifies its youth and impoverishes its widows and warehouses its elderly and deprecates the wisdom of the ones who have gone before it. Mother Jones is clear sign that no age is too late to live for justice. No season of life is too late to give the gift. No generation is without responsibility for the sins of its times.

Mother Jones was forthright and feisty. To be retiring and docile in the face of evil and the oppression of peoples was not her style. She had a truth and she said it to anyone who would listen and to those who would not. She did not cede her obligation to be a human human being to anyone. She dreamed of a better world and she set out to get it. For everyone.

PEDRO ARRUPE
The Face of Gentle Strength

It is not easy to have been born in one era and then find yourself with responsibility for the borning of one completely other than the one you have known. It takes a very special kind of person: someone embedded in the best of the past; someone totally open to the future. Liberals strive to change the future; conservatives struggle to save the past. People committed to both dimensions of life are rare breeds. They are bridge-builders as well as visionaries. They are rocks of stability in a sea of change. They are the hinges of the generations. Thanks to them we navigate dangerous waters well, make sharp curves safely, walk from one world into another with respect for both, with confidence, with sanity.

Pedro Arrupe was one of those people. In a world splitting at the seams, he was cut from both pieces of cloth.

The problem is that breakpoints in history are more a marsh of ideas than a contest of opposites. When one world view is under attack but another has not triumphed, nothing is clear; nothing is certain; nothing is the same as it used to be. To be a leader in times like these is a precarious and privileged moment. Anything can happen. Anything will.

Pedro Arrupe seemed ill-suited to the task. He was born in Spanish Basque country; he was a priest; he was a living definition of the stereotypical Jesuit: learned, self-contained, largely remote from the world of the poor or the oppressed. His world was academic and institutional. The smells of poverty and death did not easily invade and almost never contaminated the confines of libraries and chapels. And, what's more, Arrupe had been groomed for another kind of life.

Arrupe was born at the blush of a new century, in 1909, the only son of a wealthy architect. He was educated in upper-class schools. He was trained to be a physician. He was to have been a fine man of the world. Instead, the suffering he saw in medical school convinced him that what the world needed most was balm for the souls of the suffering, not simply care for the body. With that in mind, he entered the Society of Jesus, the order founded by another Basque, Ignatius of Loyola, in 1540. There he began a religious career that, in the final analysis, did indeed make him a man of the world.

When the Jesuits were suppressed in Spain during the Spanish Civil War, the young seminarian Arrupe was sent to Holland and Belgium and then to the United States to make his tertianship. Finally, in 1938, he was given permission to go to Japan, one of the most difficult mission territories in the Eastern world, where he learned the language, the culture, calligraphy, flower arrangement, and the tea ceremony. For the rest of his life the Japanese practice of squatting on a prayer mat to say his Office was his favorite position. Arrupe learned how to immerse himself in a world not his own.

But comfortably acclimated or not, Arrupe was in Japan during World War II as an undesirable alien, a Westerner. Hounded by the Japanese authorities as a spy, Arrupe spent thirty-three days in solitary confinement and learned from the experience the plight of the cultural outcast and the displaced. But he learned a great deal more than that. He learned that struggle is of the essence of justice. He learned what struggle was all about. And Arrupe needed the lesson. His entire adult life was spent in struggle: struggle with the forces of evil in the world; struggle with the renewal of religious life; struggle with the Vatican whose mission he was vowed to uphold.

The struggle with the world situation did not begin in symbol and academic speculation. Arrupe was in Hiroshima on December 7, 1941, when the United States exploded the first atom bomb on that city. The Jesuit novitiate of which Arrupe was director at that time was a healthy four miles from the center of the city, the epicenter of the explosion. Arrupe told of it later: "As I opened the door that faced the city, we heard a formidable explosion similar to the blast of a hurricane. At the same time doors, windows and walls fell upon us in smithereens." The bomb that didn't hit them had almost destroyed them. But it was then, when everything he had built seemed to have been destroyed, that everything began to come together: Arrupe the physician emerged, cleared the debris of the novitiate with the thirty-five young Jesuits with him, and turned the building into a hospital for over 150 burned and bleeding victims. When news came from the outside world that Hiroshima had just suffered the first atomic bomb, a horror with a name but no definition, word came too "not to go into the city because there was a gas over the city that would kill for seventy years." Arrupe wrote:

> It is at such times that one feels most a priest, when one knows that in the city there are 50,000 bodies that, unless they are cremated, will cause a terrible plague. There were besides some 120,000 wounded to care for. In light of these facts, a priest cannot remain outside the city just to preserve his life.

Every day Arrupe and his novices went into the area to stack and cremate corpses in hopes of averting plague.

After Hiroshima, pushing out boundaries and healing wounds never ceased to be a hallmark of Arrupe's life.

Moved to the center of his soul by the sight of the barbarity of Hiroshima, Arrupe undertook speaking tour after speaking tour to describe for a passive world the effects of technological holocaust. It was a time in which Arrupe came to know the whole world and the world him. It was also a time of religious cataclysm.

When Pedro Arrupe, the most familiar figure in the Jesuit world, was elected superior general of the Jesuits in 1965, the Second Vatican Council, which exploded the Roman Catholic Church into the twentieth century, was in its final session. A new struggle was about to begin.

Religious life, like the church out of which it sprang, had for long years, centuries even, been mired in a medieval model of asceticism and ministry. Life for the average member of a religious order was a series of pious exercises and penances and disciplines and "obediences," assignments to institutional service. Even congregations that had been founded long after the Middle Ages and the passing of the nadir of monasticism had fallen prey to routinization and institutionalism, including the Jesuits. Religious congregations that had begun among the people, in the streets, around the major issues of the day had become, for all practical purposes, quiet servants in an even quieter clerical establishment. The Jesuits, too, whose ardent scholarship and theological development had been the driving force behind the Counter Reformation and the establishment of missions in Japan, China, Latin America, and North America, had for the most part settled down to tend the educational establishments that they had begun in more challenging times in more hostile environments.

Vatican II, however, had finally unmasked the faultline in the church. The old order had passed away just when things looked their most successful, their most promising. Twenty-five percent of the religious of the world left religious life, over eight thousand from the Jesuits alone. Arrupe was entrusted with leading the order to look again at the spirit of their founder, at the needs of their members, and at the signs of the times. It was a struggle of immense proportions. To bring men on every continent to analyze — and change — a lifestyle and a mission that had become hallowed by time meant the spiritual re-education of the most educated order in the church. But Arrupe was a master at all three dimensions of renewal: he was the quintessential Jesuit, steeped in its past and immersed in its philosophy; he loved the order and the men who made it up; he read reality around him with an eye wizened by the worst barbarism of all time, the planned possibility of the nuclear suicide of the human race. Arrupe called the signs of the time poverty, hunger, oppression, and discrimination. Arrupe called the sign of the time justice. "What does it mean to be a Jesuit today?" he wrote. "It means committing oneself, under the standard of the cross, to the critical struggle of our time: The struggle for the faith, and the struggle for justice which the faith itself demands....We shall not engage in that struggle without paying a price." And indeed the price was high. Thirty-three Jesuits were murdered in the Third World in fifteen years.

Consequently, the struggle to renew Jesuit religious life at the order of the Vatican Council became a struggle with the Vatican as well, who preferred a more circumspect, a less "political" type of renewal, whatever the church's history of martyrs.

Nevertheless, in order to bring the Jesuits into contact with the culture and questions of the time, Arrupe allowed whatever experimentation was necessary. Novitiate practices were updated; seminary curriculums were enlarged; contacts across the society were broadened. Around the world, Jesuits began to use their best intellectual preparation to critique and confront unjust regimes and policies of oppression. What had been staid order became creative chaos. The criticism reached a peak: Arrupe, officials in the Roman curia said, "couldn't control his men." Arrupe had "abdicated leadership." Arrupe and the Jesuits were in a crisis, John Paul II himself told Arrupe, "causing confusion among Christian people and concern to the church, to the hierarchy, and personally to the pope." Arrupe was a man under pressure from all sides.

Arrupe's problem was that his style of leadership was collegial rather than authoritarian. He trusted his men to live in the spirit of discernment and the mission of the order. He simply could not bring himself to suppress the movement of the Holy Spirit among his brothers in the name of obedience to the system. What's more, he was himself totally committed to justice as the will of God. He accepted risk as a demonstration of faith. He refused to condemn works on behalf of justice as Marxist in inspiration, the then-current denunciation of the Jesuits by the totalitarian governments in power and by virulent anti-communists in the Vatican. In the face of Rome's attacks on Marxism Arrupe had written:

> Finally, we should also firmly oppose the efforts of anyone who wishes to take advantage of our reservations about Marxist analysis in order to condemn as Marxist or communist, or at least to minimize esteem for, a commitment to justice and the cause of the poor, the defense of their rights against those who exploit them, the urging of legitimate claims.

And then Arrupe ended the passage with the moral question of the age: "Have we not often seen forms of anti-communism that are nothing but means for concealing injustice?" A world and a church reeling from the effects of anti-colonialism knew the answer. And they did not like the question.

At the end of eighteen years of inspired leadership but unrelenting pressure, Arrupe had a

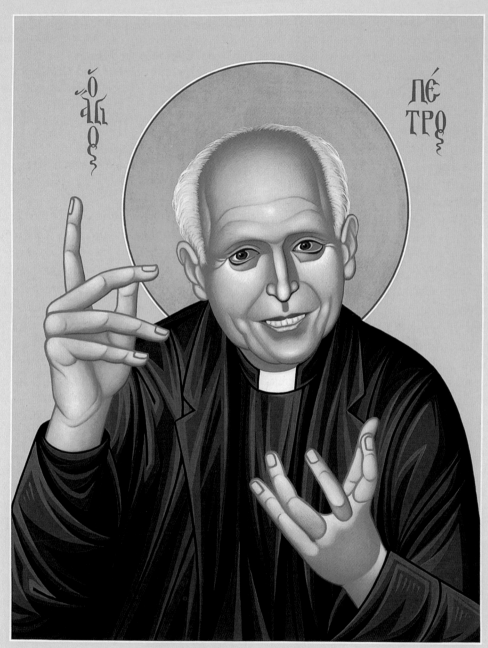

ὁ ἅγιος ΠΈΤΡΟς

DON PEDRO ARRUPE

debitating stroke after his request for papal permission to resign the position of superior general had been refused. Paralyzed and unable to speak, but alert and aware, Arrupe saw the order he had given his life to renew subjected to the control of a papal delegate, a violation of the order itself. He saw his work undermined and his loyalty to the papacy, his dearest love, impugned by the papacy itself for attempting to do what a pope and council had decreed. He saw the energy he had released around the world either dampened or redirected. Then this powerful man of the world watched mute and powerless for ten long years as the daring new Jesuit world he had brought into being was either cast into new confusion or systematically dismantled. And he did not contest it. Having done what needed to be done, he simply accepted the consequences of it and left history to judge the rightness of his actions.

Indeed, there were any number of other religious superiors in the same period, men and women, who had done the same kinds of things. The difference was that Arrupe had done it with the largest order in the world; he had done it despite the displeasure of the Roman curia; he had done it with the order closest to the papacy; he had done it around the entire world; and he had done it at the cost of lives as devoted to those principles as he was. He had succeeded at terrible cost.

Arrupe had turned an entire order around, had become a leader of renewal, a molder of thinking men, and a herald of justice for Christians far beyond the boundaries of his own congregation. Most of all, he had become the sound of significance in a world deaf to the voices of the voiceless. "Religious," he wrote in *Witnessing to Justice,* "have to foster an international, global view of humans and society. We have to make people realize that international justice, peace and solidarity are essential if we want to survive."

But Arrupe was no romantic. He knew the implications of what he was saying. He wrote further:

> In the church's preaching of the Gospel message of justice and liberation, a denunciation of existing injustices is necessarily implied....Denunciation demands courage, often great courage. For to denounce an injustice will often mean to confront, perhaps to unmask, but in any case to contradict powerful men who control the levers of economic and political power. And Christ our Lord, in the instructions He gave to His Apostles, has warned us what a risky thing it is to be a witness to the Gospel. "They will hand you over to sanhedrins and scourge you in their synagogues. You will be dragged before governors and kings for my sake, to bear witness before them and the pagans....Do not be afraid of them."

Clearly Arrupe feared nothing: not pressure from political oppressors, not unjust papal correction, not even the loss of the order. In fact, he suffered all three. In 1975, at the Jesuit General Congregation, he argued for Jesuit presence everywhere and inspired the Jesuits to become more involved in service to the poor and work for justice. He said, "If it is necessary to give witness to injustice by going to jail, well, 'welcome, jail.'"

Pedro Arrupe is a clear challenge to the church. He refounded an order on the principles of the Gospel, even over the protests of churchmen themselves. He became a beacon of conscience and commitment to religious everywhere. He became a sign of hope to Christians who wondered if the church noticed the poor at all anymore. He taught the most timid of us that there is a Law above the law that transcends all other loyalties, even our loyalty to the church. And most of all, in the face of the opposition most painful to him, the opposition of the church itself, Arrupe never backed down, never gave up, never sank into passive silence. He spoke his truth, defined his vision everywhere. He was the leader who led by going and then having the patience to wait until the rest of the world caught up.

BAAL SHEM TOV
Face of a Holy World

The world is new to us every morning – this is God's gift and each of us must believe that we are reborn every day." The words are admirable under any circumstances. What makes them most admirable, perhaps, is that when the Baal Shem Tov wrote them in eighteenth-century Poland, life for his audience of Jews there was anything but bright and bold. On the contrary, life for Jews in Poland was poor and harsh, fraught with anti-Semitism, burdened by poverty. The masses were living in misery, and Jews were most miserable of all. Hope was at a premium. It was a time for revolution, rebellion, resistance, repression, despair. The only light on the dark horizon was Hasidism.

Hasidism was a rivulet of mysticism and emotion in a people whose tradition was otherwise intellectual and prescriptive. It was a breath of feeling and simplicity for a peasant people whose life had gone dry.

The fact was that mysticism had long been suspect in the Jewish tradition. It was the Law that mattered. What was, was God's gift. Speculation in the divine, the *Mishnah* made clear, was to be discouraged. Those who "ponder over four things had better not been born," the rabbis wrote. "The four are: that which is above, that which is below, that which is before us, and that which is behind us." The teachings of Judaism were the kernel of the faith. No one was to be subverted from those by the seduction of heavenly experiences.

And yet, period after period in Jewish history, when life was more burden than blessing, the sight of the mystical consistently broke through, giving joy to lives weighted with dismay at the present.

Poland in the eighteenth century was indeed a dismal place, especially for Jews. Catholic teachings about the crucifixion of Christ by the Jews aroused — and, in its notorious simplification of the historical nature of the event, justified — an ongoing anti-Semitism. Pogroms, the malicious and unmotivated attacks on Jewish settlements, were common. Heavy public taxation ground poor peasant farmers into destitution. Education was impossible. The dark and seamy suspicion that Jews were practicing ritual murder made them outcasts in their own hometowns. To talk about human consolation, let alone divine joy, in a situation like this was at least bad taste, if not absurd. But that is exactly what the Baal Shem Tov brought to a people in pain.

Israel ben Eliezer, later known as the Baal Shem Tov, the Besht or the Master of the Good Name, was a simple man in a simple environment. He was not a Talmudic scholar. He was not a rabbi of importance. He was a man with an eye for the spiritual and a song in the heart. He left no writings, no erudite autobiography, no theological theorems. It is documented that he was born in the year 1700 and died in the year 1760.

Beyond his date of birth, however, nothing clearly authentic is known about the man. At the same time, nothing much has been forgotten about the man either. People knew he was a "Hasid" — a pious one — and that was enough for them. Around him and because of him swirled a

movement that vibrated throughout Poland and reshaped Judaism itself.

To Poland in a state of tension and Judaism awash in the dialectical study of the Torah, Israel ben Eliezer brought a new dimension of religion. Rather than simply wrestling to understand God, the Besht wanted people to experience God. Instead of looking to the hereafter for answers to the problems of life, the Baal Shem Tov wanted people to find God in the here and now. Instead of waiting for God in the world to come, the Besht insisted that the presence of God lurked in life as it was, that it was there for the seeing, that it was able to be reached and grasped and embraced — even by the poor, even by the untutored, even by the sinful. Rather than the rigors of religious observance, the Besht preached the joy of life that came from commandments kept and life well lived. Instead of fighting life, Rabbi Israel taught people to accept it with gratitude and to live it with enthusiasm.

The Baal Shem Tov taught a way of life, not a life of learning. He wrote nothing down. He was a storyteller, a teacher of parables, a provider of proverbs. Life was his text; memory was his major work. Years after the death of the Besht, it is written, the Kobriner rabbi asked the Slonimer rabbi, one of that generation's Hasids: "Have your teachers left any writings as a heritage?" On receiving an affirmative reply, the Kobriner asked: "Are they printed, or are they still in manuscript?" "Oh, neither," said the Slonimer. "They are inscribed in the hearts of their disciples."

Hasidism was like that. The disciples gathered around a zaddik, or spiritual master, whom they saw as God's guide for them in the work of salvation. They clung to his presence; they lived on his words; they breathed in his spirit and in it felt moments of redemption in the midst of labor and toil.

The Besht, the Master of the Holy Name — the one who understood the ways of God —

taught four major concepts in a world grown sad socially and depressingly solemn spiritually: that work was holy, that asceticism was self-destructive, that goodness was its own reward, and that prayer was union with God. With those four simple insights, the Besht changed the way an oppressed world saw itself and everything around it as well.

Work was not a burden to be shifted, he preached, even in a world where work bent the body and drained the soul. Work was the way the human being cooperated in the co-creation of the world. Work was a sacrament of obedience meant to glorify God and give promise to the peoples. The Hasidim taught, "Enoch was a shoemaker. As he joined the upper leather with the sole, he united God with the shehinah, the radiance of God's creating presence." Human beings, in other words, take a hand in unifying the universe, in bringing it closer to the Divine Image by working well, working hard, working purposefully. Human beings, the lesson is clear, share in the very creative act of God by the work they do to complete the world.

In a land where suffering was a given, not a choice, the Besht also taught that asceticism, far from being the hallmark and pride of the spiritual life, was actually dangerous, "dark and bitter and leading to depression and melancholy." His teaching on the subject was ungarnished: "The Glory of God reposes not where there is mourning, but only where joy in God's dictates prevails." "Asceticism," he said, "should be practiced only at the commencement of a person's self-discipline, until the evil inclinations are subdued. Later we should conduct ourselves in a normal way and be in communication with our comrades. Otherwise we will fall into pride." Joy, gratitude for the possibilities of creation in the face of its apparently barren promises, awareness of the presence of God in life that no one could take from them, the Shem Tov knew, was the best discipline for a people in darkness, a people for whom resentment was a near and menacing neighbor. The Besht taught a very

high level of spirituality to a very untutored level of people. Unlike religious teachings that prodded people into counterfeit goodness by promising them merits and rewards and levels of happiness, the Rabbi Israel taught only that goodness was its own joy, its own compensation. He taught:

> When we petition God let us ask for understanding and firmness to do God's will. Then we shall also obtain other favors in a form as unlimited as is God. We should be cautious, however, lest we be deceitful in our intention: we must not affirm that we offer prayer and acts of piety for love of God and not for anticipated rewards, whereas in our heart we remember that we will profit thereby. There is a story to the effect that a poor man asked his rich brother: "Why are you wealthy, and I am not?" The other answered: "Because I have no scruples against doing wrong." The poor brother began to misconduct himself, too, but he remained poor. He complained of this to his elder brother, who answered: "The reason your transgressions have not made you wealthy is that you did not do them from the conviction that it doesn't matter whether or not we do good or evil, but solely because you desired riches."
>
> How much more applicable is this to doing good with the proper intention!

God, the Besht taught, is not a vending machine. God is consciousness that puts everything else in life in perspective, that gives everything else in life new weight, new value.

Clearly, it was an attitude of mind the Baal Shem Tov sought to fashion, not a quest for religious trophies. He was not forming disciples to vie for some kind of point system in the next world; he was trying to change their attitudes in this one. His disciples were to seek goodness for its own sake and find therein the indomitable unflappability that being honorable assures. Or, as the disciples recorded:

> A man of piety complained to the Besht, saying: "I have labored hard and long in the service of the Lord, and yet I have received no improvement. I am still an ordinary and ignorant person." And the Besht answered: "Ah, yes, but you have gained the

realization that you are ordinary and ignorant, and this in itself is a worthy accomplishment is it not?"

Finally, the Baal Shem Tov taught the poorest of the poor and the lowest of the lowly that God was within their reach, that the achievement of God was pure joy and that every God-centered thought was prayer. He taught them to sing and dance to free themselves of the consuming distractions and the eroding passions of life that plagued them constantly so that the joy of the Lord would be their only obsession.

The Besht taught:

> The first time a thing occurs in nature, it is called a miracle; later it becomes natural, and no attention is paid to it. Let your worship and your service be a fresh miracle every day to you. Only such worship, performed from the heart, with enthusiasm, is acceptable.

And so the Hasidim, zaddiks and disciples, swayed and danced and sang and reached out with their whole bodies to the God whom they knew to be reaching back to them. "No child can be born," he taught, "except through pleasure and joy. By the same token, if we wish our prayers to bear fruit, we must offer them with pleasure and joy."

Hasidism thrived and then waned, as social movements are wont to do. The difference in this one, the difference in the Baal Shem Tov, is that he brought a whole people out of despair and depression, out of poverty and persecution, to demonstrate to the world that goodness and God are the two things that no one can take from anybody and that those two things make the human heart impenetrable, invincible, unbreakable.

Said the Besht:

> Some seek God as if God were far removed from us, and surrounded by many walls. They say, "I sought him, but I found him not." Had they been wise, however, they would have known that "no space is free of God." They can find God in everything and everywhere, and they should understand that "those who attach themselves to any part of God are as if they were attached to the All in All."

The Baal Shem Tov is an icon of the Holy World of God.

JULIAN of NORWICH
Icon of the Motherhood of God

Somewhere, someplace, a sage has written: "Those who have lived well in their own time have lived well for all time." The point is that every age needs models. Every age needs to know that people as small and fragile as themselves have carried the great burden of life and carried it well.

Models from the past encourage us in our own times. The memory of their struggle is often the light that enables us to make our small, quiet way through the murky mysteries of our own times with the same kind of courage and conviction and compassion and conscience that the great figures who have gone down similarly difficult paths before us brought to theirs.

Julian of Norwich, the fourteenth-century English anchoress, or hermit, is surprisingly enough just such a person. Like us, Julian lived through a period whose questions seared the soul. The Black Death was ravaging Europe. Mortality rates were phenomenally high. Almost half the people of England alone had fallen prey to a disease borne and bred by poverty. Mortality among the clergy was highest of all, since the chance of a priest contracting the disease was heightened by the anointing ministry to the sick. Worse, into the middle of physical plague came spiritual plague as well. The Great Schism, the Avignon papacy, with its absentee popes and its political impostors to the throne of Peter, divided the influence of the church at the very time

people were so badly in need of faith. The need for spiritual leadership, then, was keen.

In this period, too, the peasant revolts had erupted: the faltering economic situation of the poor was age-old, but, in light of the increasing expenditures of competing kings, it was now near unbearable. Julian saw that the burden of taxation fell hardest on the backs of the poor, that suffering was their lot in life, and that sin was at its base.

She lived through frequent wars whose armies did the greatest amount of damage to the agricultural communities through which they ravaged — to the people, ironically, who were least involved in the political intrigue and military machinery of their governments, the same kind of poor and vulnerable people who are the pawns of the power elites of any time.

In that period, too, wages were fixed but costs soared. Class consciousness spiraled as landlords attempted to keep the serfs and bondsmen bound to their old terms of service in order to avoid the costs of paid labor and contract work. Guilds — the unions of that day — were too often closed to new members, the very people who needed them most. The wealthy landowners of the fourteenth century, like the corporate managers of the twentieth century, often planted for quick profits and then, once the land was exhausted, abandoned those farms and left the poor out of work and out of hope. Both farm

JULIAN OF NORWICH

workers and town laborers began to know that they were being exploited and Europe was a tinder box of political tensions, an emerging new sensibility at war with an old order doomed to fall.

In France and Germany and England the peasants and lower classes of the towns rose in blind but hopeless rebellion. None of the peasant uprisings were successful, and most of them were put down ruthlessly. But the ideas were there and the ideas would not go away.

Where was God?

Who was God?

There was suffering aplenty and badly faltering faith in the course of it. Militarism and economic exploitation and social imbalance were, then as now, the policies of the powerful, the scourge of the helpless. Oh, yes, the link between the givens of that century and the struggles of this one is distressingly similar. Indeed we have need for models now. Into this environment came Julian of Norwich, a woman who was devoted only to God in an age devoted largely to things. Known as a woman of good counsel and good life in a society and a church that had both been corrupted, the fame of her spread far and wide. Her influence became a river of faith in an era weighed down by a sense of futility. Her anchorhold, the tiny hut built against the local church to which she attached herself, became a place of healing in a world full of hurt.

Julian of Norwich was a solitary who was very much connected to her time. She devoted her life to God and so she listened to people. Julian was an independent woman, a woman intent on being independent, who knew her value as a temple of God and knew God's characteristics as feminine, and taught them both. She was a spiritual guide, but she was also a personal counselor who comforted the sorrowing and discomforted the complacent — of whom her contemporaries said: "Julian has the gift of understanding."

Julian of Norwich was, in other words, a woman of social impact, of contemporary value who saw the suffering Christ in the faces of the poor and reached out to heal them. Her response to her times was simple and direct: to hear the word of God, to say it successfully, and to say it regardless of who did or who did not listen.

Julian was born in 1343, a period in which mysticism, the affective experience of God rather than the theological knowledge of God, flourished. For women especially, who had been cut off from the academic theological life of the new university system of Europe despite having operated schools of their own for centuries, mysticism became a common expression of the intensity of their God-centeredness. In fact, immersion in God and in the things of God often marked the mystics as spiritual leaders more deeply than did the academic degrees of the male churchmen around them. Julian, unlike Hildegard, who seemed to experience more a type of intellectual insight than tangible contacts with the divine, had a series of fifteen ecstatic visions — "Showings" she named them — in which she "saw" the Christ and heard revealed truths. It was the disclosure of these perceptions and their implications that made Julian a spiritual presence in her century and a mentor yet in ours.

Julian was an anchoress, "unlettered" she says of herself, though it is highly unlikely that that should be understood literally, given the depth of her allusions and the quality of her prose. Some scholars, in fact, have ranked her with Chaucer as a master of the English language. Others have explained her deprecation of her own authority as a deft device used to base her teachings on the authority of God, a far, far more irrefutable source than her own knowledge would be. Whatever the case, anchorites retired from the world to live a solitary life under a recognized rule in the spirit of the monastics of the desert. Anchorites, however, were a revival of the eremitical tradition in the midst of the city. It was a moderate, contemplative, and balanced lifestyle. The anchorite left the public world in order to appraise it from the vantage point of the mind of God. Every anchorhold was built against the side of the local church and had a swinging door to the outside world. Like the desert solitaries, anchorites, too, became a kind of public spiritual property.

Given to a life of reflection and free from the business of business or the daily demands of family, anchorites became the spiritual directors, psychotherapists, counselors, wisdom figures of the day. Julian, it seems, was especially popular.

"Never pray in a room without windows," the Talmud teaches, and Julian never lost sight of life around her. On the contrary. She was both a comfort and a challenge to everything it epitomized. In a world unraveling at the seams, she gave herself consistently to the question of why such sufferings were necessary and how God existed in the midst of such evil. She prayed for the world around her, not as a way of avoiding it but as a way of healing it, not as a mark of her distance but as a proof of her involvement. She became a person of compassion who looked on everyone and everything with the loving eyes of God. Like any good counselor, it wasn't that she did a thing about the problems brought to her, but she did strengthen the people who came so that they could. She gave spiritual support to people in physical pain. Julian was not a refuge from life; she was its mirror and its measure.

Julian and her revelations left the world with three major learnings: (1) that God is mother, (2) that fear of God is not humility, (3) that even though we sin all will be well. She left for us, in other words, a concept of the femininity of God, the accepting presence of God and total trust in God. It was no small gift to the times.

God as the harsh judge was the dominant fourteenth-century image of the role of the divine in life. In an ecclesiastical world that was defending itself from the loss of control that schisms and heresies portended, God's wrath was an effective tool in the pursuit of good order.

The teachings were clear: natural calamity was a punishment for sin; a life of penance was the agonizing price of having given in to the interests of the flesh in a world steeped in dualism. In the face of that kind of oppressive theology for oppressed people, Julian brought a breath of Love. God looks upon us, she taught, "with pity and not with blame." She went on:

> Though we sin continually God loves us endlessly, and so gently does God shew us our sin that we repent of it quietly, turning our mind to the contemplation of God's mercy, cling to this love and goodness, knowing that God is our cure, understanding that we do nothing but sin.... For if there be anywhere on earth a lover of God who is always kept safe from falling, I know nothing of it — for it was not shown me. But this was shown: that in falling and rising again we are always held close in one love. (*Showings,* chap. 82)

And then she teaches in her "Showings," how to understand the words that "sin is behovable," or in contemporary language "necessary," "inevitable," or "needs must be." She wrote

> And then God allows some of us to fall more severely and painfully than ever before — or so it seems to us. And then we (not all of whom are wise) think it was a waste of time to have started at all. It is not so, of course. We need to fall, and we need to realize this. If we never fell we should never know how weak and wretched we are in ourselves; nor should we fully appreciate the astonishing love of our Maker. In heaven we shall really and eternally see that we sinned grievously in this life: yet despite all this, we shall also see that it made no difference at all to God's love, and we were no less precious in God's sight. By the simple fact that we fell we shall gain a simple and wonderful knowledge of what God's love means. Love that cannot, will not, be broken by sin, is rock-like, and quite astonishing. It is a good thing to know this. Another benefit is the sense of insignificance and humbling that we get by seeing ourselves fall. Through it, as we know, we shall be raised up to heaven: but such exaltation might never have been ours without the prior humbling. We have got to see this. If we do not, no fall would do us any good. Normally, we fall first, and see afterward — and both through God's mercy. (*Showings,* chap. 61)

Julian's immortal sentence of hope, then, becomes clear, and those who have spent all their lives struggling to live into the love of God, burdened always by the weight of their own existence, understand it best: "And Jesus answered with these words and said, 'Sin is necessary, but all shall be well, and all shall be well, and all manner of things shall be well.'" It is through our sins that we grow. It is through our sins that we turn ourselves toward God. It is through our sins that we come to recognize the place of God in our lives. It is a theology that raises us to the divine through the weakest elements of our humanity. It is an alleluia to life.

Finally, Julian makes her most original contribution to mystical literature. She not only uses feminine imagery to refer to God, and Jesus, but she explains it theologically. Julian teaches a patriarchal church and a machismo world in the *Showings*:

> As truly as God is our Father, so truly is God our Mother, and God revealed that in everything, and especially in these sweet words where God says: I am he; that is to say: I am he, the power and goodness of fatherhood; I am he, the wisdom and the lovingness of motherhood; I am he, the light and the grace which is all blessed love; I am he, the Trinity; I am he the unity....
>
> I understand three ways of contemplating motherhood in God. The first is the foundation of our nature's creation; the second is his taking of our nature, where the motherhood of grace begins; and the third is the motherhood at work.
>
> ...The mother can give her child to suck of her milk, but our precious Mother Jesus can feed us with himself, and does, most courteously and most tenderly, with the blessed sacrament, which is the precious food of true life.

Julian of Norwich was a theological light, a sign of hope, a voice of divine love, in a world gone sour with corruption in the church, chaos in the state, plague in the physical world, and unrest in the social order. She was an arrow, a plumbline, a beacon. She was testimony to a better way.

Clearly, in a world where systems still exist for themselves rather than for the people they are meant to serve and a permanent underclass of poor has been created for the convenience of the rich, there is much to be learned here.

Julian of Norwich belongs to a new time as a simple witness of God's love in the face of human futility, full of faith, full of challenge, full of personal responsibility, believing surely that God's spirit is in all of us and begging us to set it free.

Her simple life leaves a profoundly simple message. A story is told of a traveler who found a small bird lying upside down on its back. "Bird," the traveler said, "why are you lying upside down like that?"

"I heard the heavens are going to fall today," the bird replied.

"I suppose," the traveler laughed, "you think your spindly little legs are going to hold it up."

And the little sparrow said quietly, "Well, Sir, one does what one can."

Julian of Norwich did for her time what she could and what it needed. She gave it insight and trust and hope. We would do well to do the same.

OSCAR ROMERO
Icon of Ordinariness

The truth is that he simply did not seem the type. Correction: It wasn't that he didn't "seem" the type; it was that he really was not the type. On the contrary: Oscar Romero was the real thing. He was a real peasant, a real company man, a real patriot, a real bishop. He was the ultimate defender of the status quo, a lover of law and order, a spiritual leader, not a social activist, a true believer in the pastoral rather than the prophetic – read "political" – nature of the priesthood. In fact, he had been made a bishop for those very reasons. Yet, before it was over, they killed him as a subversive, an enemy of the state, an agitator. Which means that it could happen to anyone. Even to you and me.

Interestingly enough, it is always when churches claim to be the least "political" that they are the most beholden to the political system. Oscar Romero was an archexample. Like most of us, he believed in the system. And, like for most of us, the system betrayed his trust. If they ever had a willing pawn in their lives, they had one in Oscar Romero. To drive this man from trusting obedience to the civil system would require the state to do something outrageous. And it did. And so did the U.S. government. The only difference was that Romero saw that it was outrageous and we did not.

The United States Central Intelligence Agency analysts concluded in 1980 that the Catholic Church in El Salvador had "recently tilted officially to the extreme left." But Salvador is a place of extremes. According to U.S. political scientists, El Salvador has the "most rigid class structure and the worst income inequality in all of Latin America." Even now, less than 2 percent of the population owns more than 60 percent of the land, including most of the coffee plantations, and coffee is the country's chief export and so the country's chief income-producing product. The poorest 20 percent of the population own no land at all and receive only 2 percent of the national income. Since 1931, the time of the first peasant uprisings, the country has been ruled almost exclusively by military governments that have responded to political unrest with violent repression. The fourteen families comprising the oligarchy that owns and rules El Salvador include only a few thousand people in a country of almost five million, but they receive 50 percent of the national income.

El Salvador, in other words, is a country of serfs in the twentieth century, a cauldron of discontent, a hotbed for revolution, and a breeding ground for communism. It is also, therefore, the focus of a U.S. foreign policy determined to squelch any hint of socialism

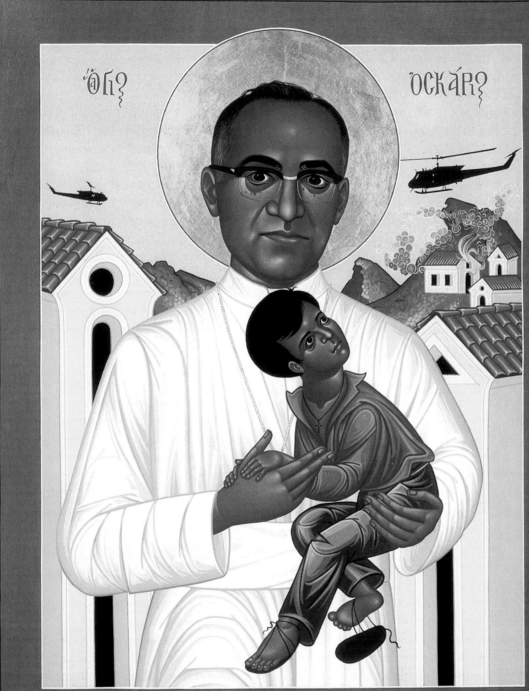

ΟϹΚΆΡϹ

OSCAR ROMERO DE EL SALVADOR

on its capitalist borders. Poverty or no poverty, the United States decreed, El Salvador was not to be a Nicaragua. It was to stay what it was so that the United States could stay what it was, and at any price to anybody.

The situation, then, seems open and shut. At least for the romantics and the idealists among us: El Salvador was a land of massive injustice. The church would obviously have no choice but to speak out. But there were many who thought otherwise and Oscar Romero was definitely one of them.

Oscar Romero was born in a small, rural village, Ciudad Barrios, in southern El Salvador in the year 1917. He was a pious boy from a large family who preferred prayer and study to the carpentry for which he was apprenticed. At the age of thirteen he went to the minor seminary in San Miguel, a seven-hour ride by horseback from his town down a winding mountain trail. From that trip on, however, it was uphill all the way for Oscar Romero. The peasant boy from the small village at the top of a Central American mountain went from the tiny seminary in San Miguel to Gregorian University in Rome for a doctorate in ascetical theology. Along with the study of sanctity, his prayer life deepened and so did his commitment to the church that formed it.

In El Salvador, a country of few priests and many Catholics, he rose rapidly in the ecclesiastical ranks, an efficient performer, a dedicated worker, a trusted official. He ran a gamut of church offices — secretary of the diocese, pastor of the cathedral parish, secretary general of the National Conference of Bishops, editor of the diocesan newspaper, rector of the seminary. Romero was an obedient priest. What he was told to do, he did, and his reputation as a no-nonsense, hard-hitting, church loyalist grew rapidly. What was even more meaningful, however, was that he did not approve of what he considered irresponsible interpretations of Vatican II and he did approve of Opus Dei, the rapidly growing right-wing of the post-Vatican II

church. He continually corrected what he judged to be the excesses of Vatican II; he chose a spiritual director from Opus Dei. He was "safe" in doctrine, and he believed that personal conversion was the essence of the priestly life, not public works.

He was the perfect choice for bishop.

He did not disappoint a church concerned with a breakdown in order. He did not disappoint a government intent on maintaining the blessing of the church while it silenced the voices of the poor. Romero moved quickly to bolster the Old Order in both: he wrote an editorial publicly condemning the social involvement of priests; he removed the Jesuits from the diocesan seminary; he sent a report to Rome outlining three factors contributing to "the politicization of the priesthood." Each move struck another blow at social change and gave the government another weapon in its war against the poor but restless peasants of El Salvador.

On May 23, 1973, his editorial in *Orientactión*, the diocesan newspaper, launched an attack on the local Jesuit high school and denounced the "demagoguery and Marxism" found in "the pamphlets and literature, of known Red origin, in a certain school." The next day the secular papers took up the cry of "Marxism" and unleashed an investigation of Jesuit education. In the end, the school was vindicated, but the theme of a Marxist priesthood had been sounded for years to come.

Thanks to Romero's aggressive public assault, the Jesuits were forced out of the seminary by the National Conference of Bishops, by unanimous vote, because of the theology they taught and the practices they permitted, and Romero himself was installed as its rector. Within a year the seminary had failed, but the reactionary tone of church formation had been set.

In the document "Three Factors in the Priests' Political Movement in El Salvador," his memorandum to the Pontifical Commission for Latin America to which he had been named as a consulter, Romero cited the Jesuits and their "political theology," the inter-diocesan justice and peace commission and its "biting and negative criticism against the capitalists and the government," and, finally, the "groups of priests and religious" who were operating peasant development centers and arguing that the church could not be apolitical. The greatest concern of Latin American bishops, Romero maintained in the memorandum, was "the spiritualizing of the clergy." Rome, thanks in part at least to Romero, was confirmed in its worst fears: communism was infiltrating the church itself. Drastic measures were in order.

There was no doubt that Romero was a good man, a caring priest, and an upstanding bishop. He decried evil and did charity. But though Romero was a pastor indeed, he was definitely not a prophet. To Romero, the church was to transcend the world, to define its values, but never, ever to concern itself with its affairs. When he became archbishop of San Salvador in 1977, he was the comfort of a conservative episcopacy and the darling of a rich people's government perhaps, but he was anything but the hope of the poor. Yet three years later, he was assassinated on their behalf. What happened? What does such a turn of events say to the rest of us?

So sure was the government of the innocuousness of the new archbishop that they launched a massacre of priests the very week of his installation as bishop of the diocese. Priests had been murdered before, of course, even in Romero's own diocese of Santiago de María, but Romero's protests had been both secret and polite, respectful and restrained. Politically proper and ignored. Oh, he had deplored the situation, of course, but gingerly. The left he accused of specific sins; the right he exhorted to charity. The right he called to be kind; the left he told that they were bringing violence on themselves because of their refusal to cooperate with the government. After all, he reasoned, it wasn't the

affair of the church; he was not sure of the motives of the victims; it was better to talk to the officials directly than to stir up public unrest.

The problem, it seems, is that churches are not easily converted. The United States, for instance, was a land of slavery for hundreds of years but the church did not speak out; the United States waged a brutal and illegal war against the land and the innocent people of Vietnam, but the church did not speak out; the United States created the end of the world and planted it in the cornfields of Kansas, but it took forty-five years for the U.S. church to begin to speak out. Not only was the church in El Salvador no different, but Oscar Romero was no different either. For Romero, priest and bishop of the diocese of San Salvador, the preservation of the institutional church was a far more important consideration than the protection of the people of the country. Romero was an institution man, good, faithful, docile, and supportive of the establishments of church and state. Very supportive. But in San Salvador things changed for Romero. This time they killed Rutilio Grande, a Jesuit whom Romero had known personally and judged to be "not like the others," passionate in his commitment to the plight of the poor but "balanced," "sensible." Rutilio, Romero knew for himself, was not Marxist; he was simply Christian to the core. Romero was stunned, overwhelmed, enraged by the murder. This was not law; this was not defense of the state; this was not the system he was beholden to obey. This was persecution of the church. This was the trampling of the People of God. This was evil. And he was bishop.

No one knows exactly what changed Romero. No one knows if it was immediate or long in coming. Was it that the accumulation of violence over the years had finally reached a saturation point in him? Was it the sight at last of the body of a friend lying on the garbage heap of bodies that had become such a common sight in El Salvador that moved him? Was it the blinding grace of a genuinely new vision that made him see again what he had seen before but see it differently?

Or was it perhaps the very values that had always driven him come together in one decisive moment that impelled him to change: the power of all those years of prayer, the futility of all those years of temporizing in the name of spirituality, the impact of all those years of poverty, the emptiness of all those words about the nature of the church and the meaning of the Gospel — lived until this moment in him almost exclusively as intellectual concepts. Was the change in him triggered by the fact that the words had now become translated into the eucharistic sacrifice of real people and into the wounds of his own torn heart that finally erupted like a storm in the man? Whatever it was that moved him most, he knew suddenly that what was, was wrong and he knew his own obligations to set it right. He knew that charity without justice was not Good News at all. He knew that to preach the reign of God to come without demonstrating the reign of God among us was at best a vapid and an empty witness, a farce without promise. Whatever it was, he knew it now and there was no stopping him.

Oscar Romero became a light to the nations, a man on fire, a prophet's prophet.

In the face of fierce breaches of divine law in a Catholic country, Romero began to break a few laws himself, to become a counterweight to a civil system that called itself righteous by becoming a living symbol of the righteousness of God: he suspended every Mass in the diocese with the exception of the Mass at the cathedral in order to create a major demonstration of the power of the people while he preached in public about the sins of the government. The rich complained that this was an infringement on their faith because they would not be able to get to Mass, and the secretary to the papal nuncio reminded him coldly about canon law, but Romero did it anyway and told the people why. In one dramatic move, it galvanized the people behind a leader and the priests and nuns behind a shepherd. It also put the government on notice.

He encouraged the priests to help the poor in their efforts to organize into opposition groups and labor unions and defended them for doing it. He boycotted government events himself to show his disapproval of the regime. He held diocesan study days on the relationship of the Gospel to the social situation. He listened and listened and listened to his priests and to his people. And he learned.

Through it all, he went to the funerals of one murdered church worker after another, their priests murdered with them.

> I rejoice, brothers and sisters, that our church is persecuted precisely for its preferential option for the poor, and for seeking to become incarnate in the interests of the poor.... How sad it would be, in a country where such horrible murders are being committed, if there were no priests among the victims! A murdered priest is a testimonial of a church incarnate in the problems of the people. ...A church that suffers no persecution, but enjoys the privileges and support of the powers of this world — that church has good reason to be afraid! But that church is not the true church of Jesus Christ.

He went to the city dumps during the day to search for the bodies of the missing. He did a radio program that named the dead and comforted the beaten and excoriated the system. So popular and so fearsome were the programs that stores reported record sales of earphones to people who wanted to hear the sermons but were afraid to be known to have done so.

He discovered the relationship between the economic system, military repression, and the plight of the peasants for whom there was no work from harvest to harvest and who were exploited even then. "The situation is so bad," he said in an interview in *Prensa Latina*, "that the faith itself has been perverted; the faith is being used to defend the financial interests of the oligarchy."

He recognized the role of the United States in the military oppression of his people, and he decried it, too, when we neither saw nor spoke to it ourselves. He wrote an open letter to President Jimmy Carter begging him to stop the military aid that was being used to repress, murder, and exterminate the poor: "If this newspaper report is correct," he wrote,

> your government's contribution [of military equipment and advisors], instead of favoring the cause of justice and peace in El Salvador, will surely increase injustice here and sharpen the repression that has been unleashed against the people's organizations fighting to defend their most fundamental human rights.

But U.S. taxpayer money went on subsidizing the slaughter of Salvadoran poor.

He was fearless: he talked about the terror designed to leave the poor powerless to respond:

> If we should oblige them, they will have won. But I do not believe the murder of these five [churchworkers] has been in vain. They have preceded us in the experience of the resurrection. We live by that power that even death cannot destroy. We honor them and our faith by living unafraid, by knowing that evil has no future.

In the end, he paid the consequence for saying the truth in the light. The church of privilege, his brother bishops, ignored him as many do to this day, in fact, and reported him to Rome for three straight apostolic visitations. This was the blow that hurt him most, he once told friends in tears. The rich waged million-dollar ad campaigns against him in the hope of precipitating his mental breakdown. The government taunted him and threatened him and hounded him and

ringed him round with violence till on March 24, 1980, they killed him, too. But the people took heart and found hope in a church for whom the Beatitudes were real. Real.

Oscar Romero is a frightening figure if for no other reason than that he shows us to ourselves. The problem is that there is an Oscar Romero lurking in all of us docile, trusting, and obedient people. He teaches us that we too may someday have to change, not because we do not believe in the teaching of the church and the state, but precisely because we do and they are not living up to it.

Indeed, Romero was a loyalist who became a voice of truth to the system he dearly wanted to serve. He was a pastor who discovered that binding wounds is no substitute for eliminating them. He was a quiet person too honest to stay silent forever. He was a Christian who discovered that the Gospel supersedes the church.

He told the people:

> If they ever take our radio [which was being bombed and jammed], suspend our newspaper, silence us, put to death all of us priests, bishop included, and you are left alone—a people without priests—then each of you will have to be God's microphone. Each of you will have to be a messenger, a prophet. The church will always exist as long as even one baptized person is left alive!

Oscar Romero calls the ordinary Christian to extraordinary heights and proves that the prophetic is possible in all of us.

ΗΑΓΙΑ ΕΔΙΘ

EDITH STEIN von OSWIECIM

EDITH STEIN
The Prescience of God

I t is one thing to ride the tide of history awash in newly emerging awarenesses. It is one thing to be carried by the tide of a public so engulfed in the throes of social change that it is almost necessary to be avant-garde, clearly chic to be different, often applauded to be revolutionary. It is another thing entirely to brave the social flow alone and to go always in its opposite direction. Edith Stein was one of those figures in life who made the way before us, by herself, in the face of overwhelming odds. Edith Stein was a Jew in Hitler's Germany, a brilliant woman in a man's world, a Catholic nun from the Jewish synagogue.

She was out of step everywhere. She didn't look like a candidate for Christianity but she was; she didn't look like the martyr type, but she was; she didn't look like the stuff of which feminists are made, but she was.

Edith Stein was raised to be a practicing Jew. She died a practicing Catholic caught in the Jewish Holocaust. At first scan, her early posture and her final plight seem cruel and unconnected. At base, however, the two stances were actually one. Edith Stein, the Jewess, was born on the feast of Yom Kippur, the Day of Atonement for sin. Edith Stein, the Catholic nun called Sister Teresa Benedicta de Cruce, never doubted for a moment that she was meant to atone for the Christian sin that exterminated six million Jews.

Edith Stein bore in her own body the two great oppressions of her time: she was female in a sexist society and Jewish in an anti-Semitic one. The one blocked her from the intellectual centers of Europe; the other cost her her life. But that has happened to a number of people in life. The death camps were filled, surely, with smart Jewish women who had never been allowed to function in a man's world and who were being killed simply because they were Jewish. The difference with Edith Stein is that she dealt with both her femaleness and her Jewishness consciously and so forced the rest of the world to do the same. The sense of isolation and inner loneliness that came with being different, being other, being rejected for all the wrong reasons plagued Stein all her life. But because of them, she became the saint-of-the-in-between-times. She was always one thing when she was expected to be another and so showed us all that the second dimension was possible. She was an intellectual, and though she was never really admitted into the academy, she refused to relinquish the scholarly life. She was a Christian but was loyal to her Jewishness to the very end. She was a woman who refused to be less than she could be simply because she was not a man.

She was also a somewhat unremarkable personality. Classmates remember her as a bright person but a basically colorless one. A college friend wrote of her,

> Edith Stein passed completely unnoticed among us in spite of a reputation for exceptional intelligence. She even seemed old-fashioned to us ...always seated in the first row of the class, a small thin figure, insignificant and seemingly absorbed in the intensity of her thought. She wore her smooth dark hair parted down the middle and twisted in back in a long knot. She had an almost sickly pallor, and her large black eyes with their intense gaze appeared stern and almost distant, as though to divert importunate curiosity.... She cannot be said to have been beautiful or pretty, nor did she possess that feminine charm which captivates hearts from the first. But there was something incomparable in this countenance... — a peaceful radiance which one never wearied of beholding.

On the other hand, she was anything but indistinguishable intellectually. The young scholar who would later be denied a university position because she was a woman was the favorite pupil and teaching assistant of Edmund Husserl, the founder of twentieth-century phenomenology. And the discipline stood her well. The fact was that religion, too, was a reality not to be scorned, a phenomenon not to be flippantly dismissed. When Max Scheler, a philosophy professor for whom Stein had great respect, returned to the Catholic faith, Stein wrote that

> his thought revealed a universe until then totally unknown to me....It discovered for me a domain of phenomena which I could not henceforth ignore. It is not in vain that we learned to set aside all bugbears and to welcome everything without prejudice. Thus it happened that I went beyond the confines of the rationalism in which I had been reared without realizing it and found myself suddenly in the world of faith. I saw dwelling there under my own eyes persons I respected and with whom I was in daily contact. This fact merited reflection.

It was the autobiography of Teresa of Avila, the story of a strong woman who had had multiple opportunities to lose herself in the trivial but who had forsworn them all for the life of the spirit, that finally brought Edith Stein to the moment of conversion from Judaism to Roman Catholicism. Yet, in some ways, she was never converted at all. She was simply transmuted from one measure of the spiritual life to another.

The Steins were devout and practicing Jews. The laws were sacred; the rituals binding. For Edith, however, God had been a remote and impersonal force for years, not a personal one. This personal God she found in Catholicism, where the mystical life and the image of Christ were more tangible than the traditions. At the same time, Edith Stein remained Jewish to the end and saw one manifestation of faith inextricably linked to the other. So certain was she of the many faces of truth that to the person who sought to console her at the time of her mother's death by suggesting that old Mrs. Stein had converted to

Catholicism on her deathbed, Edith answered firmly: "The unwavering faith which sustained her entire life did not fail her at the moment of death. I believe that this faith permitted her to triumph over the torments of agony and earned for her the treasure of mercy of a judge with whom she is now my most faithful support. May her intercession help me to reach my goal." It was an ecumenical confession of faith during a period of violent racial tension and unapologetic theological claims by supporters of the dogmas of the True Church.

The situation was only symbolic of a more universal trait, however. Edith Stein was always, and in every way, just one step out of sync with her times, one step ahead of common consciousness.

In classical Germany, her philosophy of education dealt with social responsibility as well as cultural achievement. She took for salary only the amount of money she needed to live. She fed poor families every day. She organized her students into social action teams.

In a period of widespread agnosticism she remained a believer in the human soul and for that reason left the study of cognitive psychology in order to find meaning in life.

In a culture that denied her the academic positions to which her credentials entitled her, first because she was a woman and later because she was a Jew, she became the most published woman of her time and a scholar of enduring quality.

In a world that took the subservience of women as a theological given, Edith Stein argued that theology on its own terms. In her essay "The Vocation of Man and Woman according to Nature and to Grace," Stein wrote:

> The first words of Holy Scripture that treat of [human beings] assign a common vocation to both.... Both together are given a threefold task: They are to be the image of God, to produce posterity, and to rule the earth. Nothing is said here

about this threefold vocation being carried out by each of them in a different way.... There is no question here of a dominion of man over woman. She is called his companion and help, and the man is told that he will cleave to her and they will both be one flesh.

And then she goes on to critique the Pauline letters so commonly used as proof of the secondary role of women:

> Here [in the First Letter to Timothy] even more strongly than in the Letter to the Corinthians, one has the impression that the original order and the redemptive order are subordinated by the order of fallen nature.... What is said here and what may have been feasible concerning certain improprieties of the Greek community is not to be considered as binding for the principal teachings on the relationship of the sexes. It contradicts too strongly the words and the whole custom of the Lord who had women among his closest companions and who showed at every turn in His redemptive work that He was as much concerned about the soul of woman as the soul of man.

Theology and scripture, she insisted, were themselves proof of the equality of women. And clearly she believed it.

In a church where men controlled the sacraments and defined the dogmas and wrote the laws and occupied, almost without challenge, all the positions of the church in the name of God's will for them, Edith Stein had the effrontery to ask for an appointment with a pope in order to call the church from its passive role in Nazi Germany to active support for the Jews. She was, of course, denied the audience, but her words only rang truer in the wake of that denial. She had insisted in "The Ethos of Women's Professions":

> Only subjective delusion could deny that women are capable of practicing vocations other than that of spouse and mother. The experience of the last decades, and for that matter, the experience of all times, has demonstrated this.... And there is no profession which cannot be practiced by a woman. ...But, also, individual gifts and tendencies can lead to the most diversified activities. Indeed, no woman is only "woman" – like a man, each has

her individual specialty and talent, and this talent gives her the capability of doing professional work, be it artistic, scientific, technical....

However, over and above this, one may say that even the professions whose objective requirements are not harmonious with feminine nature, those termed as specifically masculine, could yet be practiced in an authentically feminine way if accepted as part of the concrete human condition....

Thus the participation of women in the most diverse professional disciplines could be a blessing for the entire society, private or public, precisely if the specifically feminine ethos would be preserved.

It was a position years ahead of its time.

Finally, in a world where a Christian nation tolerated the extermination of Jews, the Christian Jew, Edith Stein, went to her death as a Jew atoning for Christian sin of barbarous proportion. It was not a heroic staging. Edith Stein did not devise her death to make a point; she simply accepted it. The facts of the case were pathetically simple: Edith had entered the Carmelite monastery in Cologne. A few years later, her sister Rosa, also a convert to Catholicism, had joined her there. Both of them had been sent from the Carmel in Cologne to the Carmelite monastery in Holland to escape the growing anti-Semitism of Germany. At Echt in Holland, ironically, the bishops of the church had taken the stand that Stein had wanted from the pope. They had written a pastoral condemning Nazi socialism. Now Jews in Holland were in imminent danger. This time a Carmel in Switzerland agreed to take Edith but, unaware apparently of the gravity of the situation, said that they had no room for Rosa as well. In the last principled decision of her life, Edith refused to accept a refuge that had no place for her sister too. Attempts were continued to find a place for both of them but the efforts were either too casual or too slow. Within a week of the release of the bishops' pastoral letter to the churches, German soldiers rounded up fifteen hundred Jewish converts to Christianity in

retaliation for public criticism by the church and sent them all to the ovens of Auschwitz.

Edith Stein died in Auschwitz one week after her arrival there. She went to her death peacefully, and she embraced it in an attitude of atonement. She may have been the only Christian alive who fully realized the impact of what it meant in those days to be both Christian and Jew.

When Edith Stein was canonized by the Catholic Church, Jews in large numbers resented the act itself. Edith Stein did not die for the Catholic faith, they argued; Edith Stein died because she was a Jew. Perhaps, the church answered, but if she had not been a Jewish Christian, she would most likely have been alive today. The debate is a useless one. The fact is that Edith Stein is not important because she was martyred for anything. Edith Stein is not a light to take into the twenty-first century because she was killed by Nazis for whatever reason. Edith Stein is a pathway through darkness because of the courage it takes to critique your own. She saw always what was in front of her and she said what she saw, leaving the chips to fall where they would. She is sign to a new generation because of her ability to accept life and death with equal confidence. Edith Stein is eternal flame and endless day because she was a brilliant and successful person for whom brilliance and success were not enough. Edith Stein is a tribute to loyalty, to honesty in the face of dulling barbarity, to the spiritual in the face of a world that worshiped the material, to brave virtue in a world that cultivated lies.

She wrote once, "Those who truly love their neighbor will not be unsympathetic and apathetic to their neighbor's need. Words should inspire action; otherwise, words are mere rhetoric camouflaging nothingness, concealing merely empty or illusory feeling and opinions." It is a sobering reminder yet from an icon of the prescient will of God.

MARTIN of TOURS
Holy Disobedience

It's never easy to reach back into another century, to really understand its political texture, to appreciate its struggles, to grasp its emotional climate. The language and style of other periods put us off, the circumstances lose in translation, the intrigues seem paltry in the face of the international commerce and global controls of today. The fourth century, however, the century of Martin of Tours, has a kind of eerie familiarity.

The official persecution of Christians was barely over before Martin of Tours tested the social situation with his refusal to serve in the army of the emperor. The two kingdoms of the East and West had only recently been reunited under the throne of Constantine the Great. The Edict of Milan establishing toleration for Christians was still fresh news to the political scene. The first basilican church of Rome acknowledging the public legitimacy of Christianity had been built just a few years before. Gladiatorial combats had only recently been outlawed.

Clearly, the face of Europe was changing. The soul of Europe was up for auction. Political alliances had shifted. The church had become a public institution. All in all, it was a time not unlike our own. In our time, too, East-West tensions consumed the government. War became a holy act, a doctrine of the civil religion. No price was too high to pay, no horror was too inhuman to imagine to preserve the power of the state. The world divided itself between the pious and the impious. But when Japan surrendered and later when the Berlin Wall fell and Communism became a market economy, people who had once been called demonic were received into the international fold, all their sins forgiven, all their vices forgotten.

In the midst of it all the Roman church, once rejected in the United States as dangerously papist, proved its mettle by the number of its sons who died to demonstrate their patriotism and the loyalty of Catholic citizens. Instead of crucifixes, Catholic parishes hung the names of their war dead in the vestibules of their churches to equate the death of those in battle with the death of the One on the cross. Bishops blessed bombers and military chaplains donned the uniform of the country. For years the National Conference of Catholic Bishops said not a word about the war in Vietnam while bishops dined at White House banquets and gave private solace to the president. It was a time of church-state seduction of the highest quality. And then with thousands in their wake, the Berrigan brothers, Dan and Phil, one a Jesuit and the other a Josephite, appeared on the scene. They were priests who said that war was wrong and the government immoral to spend the blood of its young on the destruction of others, and they threw both church and state into confusion.

The state found itself with a body of dissenters who based their opposition to the war on religions that had themselves been the greatest preachers of obedience "to lawful authority." The church that had touted the just war theory on every side of every war found itself confronted with a stream of believers who claimed pacifism as a legitimate and basic and honorable tradition in the church. And they cited Martin of Tours, a Christian of the fourth century, as one of their sources and one of their models. Few could have predicted the intersection of the fourth century with the twentieth century but the fit was unmistakable.

Martin of Tours, like many young Americans even now, came from a military family and lived in a military world. His father was a cavalry officer under the Roman emperor Constantine the Great. Martin was an army child, born in Hungary, raised in northern Italy, bred for the corps. His future was to have been a clear one. As the son of an army officer, he would automatically be conscripted into the army. It was the law. It was his lineage. It was his role in society.

The problem was that Martin had begun to see the world differently from his parents and the people around them. The values of the war machine had ceased to persuade. The peaceful Christ rather than Mars, the god of war for whom he was named, began to be his ideal. The kingdom of God, rather than the Roman Empire, fired the imagination and gripped the soul of a young man for whom the world in which he was raised no longer seemed to define what it meant to be a real human being. Martin resisted the army, his head filled with ideas about desert monastics who lived life without money and without power and who were opposed to the soft and slippery ways of the world around them.

In the end, it was his own father who saw the makings of a deserter in his son. It was the military father who had his own son picked up and taken away forcibly to the base where he would do his duty, where he would come to his senses, where he would learn to be a man. Translation: where he would learn to be a loyal pawn of the state and a certified national robot.

Then it happened. Martin was faced with the ultimate decision and he made it. In 341 near Worms, when the forces of the empire were about to attack the Franks, the officers called the soldiers of Martin's regiment together, as was the custom in Roman armies the night before a major battle, to receive the donative, the emperor's bonus or gift to servicemen for war-time pay. But Martin refused it. He looked at the emperor, early sources claim, and said, "Before this I have made war for you; now let me make war for God. Let the ones who will fight take the donative."

The response to Martin's position was to be expected in a society where Christians were still an oddity and being Roman was still a privileged state. The army did what any males do who have been raised to prove their manliness by brutality: they called Martin a coward. "I'm a soldier of Christ," he said. "I cannot fight." And then, to make the distinction between Christianity and cowardice, he volunteered to stand in front of the enemy unarmed. There was only one thing he would not do. He would not raise a weapon against another. He would not coerce the weak. He would not force the fearful. He would not kill.

They didn't call it civil disobedience in those days. They called it treason. They called it apostasy. They shunted him out of the corps.

Eventually, Martin gathered a community of monastics around him, men whose whole lives stood in direct opposition to the male values of the world in which they had been formed, to remind their world of the gentle, loving, saving Christ.

It seems so long ago now. It seems so remote. It seems so very unrelated. It seems that there is nothing here to engage us sixteen centuries later except the dim memory of an early saint, the frail memory of a person renowned among early masses but little defined, a substanceless shadow of another era. It seems that there is little here to care about.

But we care about war. We spend more on the military than any other nation on earth. No people in the history of humankind has spent so much money on "defense" and by that very action made themselves so vulnerable. The Christianity of Martin of Tours, who met the demands of the peacemaking Christ, challenges us more than ever today to think newly about war.

We care about civic life. We pride ourselves on the American Way and the American Dream. The life of Martin of Tours goads us to challenge civic life to standards far and above civic virtues. We care about the ideals of citizenship. We make laws to guard the flag of the country. We wage long election campaigns to produce a popular vote. We call ourselves a democracy and then bear the crippling effects of one national corruption after another. The life of Martin of Tours prods us to a citizenship that dares to question the nature of citizenry itself.

We care about social approval and fear to upset dinner conversations and church socials and cocktail parties with the hard questions of life and the glare of public actions. The life of Martin of Tours models for us what it takes to brave the jeering masses in our own worlds, in our own neighborhoods, in our own church, in our own families.

We care about the role of Christianity in the world today. The life of Martin of Tours challenges us to care more for the church as prophetic witness than for the church as socially safe and pitiably respected institution.

Indeed, our kind too, our kind most of all perhaps, needs a Martin of Tours, an icon of the convicting face of a gentle God.

THOMAS MERTON
Icon of the Voice of God

The public psychoanalysis of Thomas Merton has proceeded at a steady pace for twenty years. His life, his family, the circumstances that influenced his development, his motives and motivations have been dissected beyond belief. The picture of the man that emerges is, nevertheless, a blurred one at best. Was he the sad product of a psychologically cold and remote mother? Or was he the less talented son of an artist father? Was he a monk who was never given the space he needed to live the life he wanted? Or was he a public figure who was never able successfully to be a monk? Was he a frustrated hermit or was he a social figure of almost electric magnetism?

The answers are all interesting, of course. At one level, they are even immensely important. If a young *roué* can turn into a hermit, there is hope for the part of all of us that is out of control. If an educated agnostic can become a theologian of superior measure, our own recurring doubts and nagging questions and irrepressible uncertainties cease to loom so large in the appraisal of our spiritual lives. If a monk can take on a public character, none of us is allowed to plead powerless. If, after twenty-six years in monastic life, a solemnly professed Cistercian can still be questioning his vocation, flirting with marriage, falling in love, then the rest of us can stumble from period to period in life as well, unsure sometimes of what really anchors us, perhaps, but very sure of our sincere commitment to become what we are.

Indeed, Thomas Merton's patchwork life is a comfort to the average person. It is at the same time a confusion. Merton was a precocious child, an out-of-control youth, a dissipated young man, a college playboy, an intellectual. Thomas Merton was not the boy next door. He was a man who walked the path from hell to heaven, exposing the journey at every turn so that the rest of us could find hope and meaning in our own.

Yet the Thomas Merton who will be remembered will not be remembered for any of the details of his life, fascinating though they are. He was born in France in 1915, the first son of Ruth Jenkins and Owen Merton, art students in Paris, and spent his early life between a small village in France and, with Europe on the brink of war, at his grandparents' home on Long Island. By the time he was six, his mother had died. After that, home was a series of places both here and abroad where his father went to paint. Tom became a citizen of the world with roots nowhere and restrictions few. His father lived the artist's life; young Tom lived it, too. The only religion he knew was the stuff of oil paintings and church architecture and peasants who practiced the faith, whose lives were the only Gospel Merton ever learned but to whose memories he turned in later years for living models of the spiritual world. By the age of sixteen, Merton was an orphan who had watched his father die an inch at a time from a brain tumor. Suffering had become a senseless but steady part of his young world and comfort a goddess to be pursued. A brilliant student, Merton managed to flunk out of Cambridge University after nights of partying and days full of idleness. He had fathered a child and become known for his carousing. He wrote later of those years, "Everything I had reached out for turned to ashes in my hands.... I myself, in the bargain, had turned out to be an extremely unpleasant sort of person — vain, self-centered, dissolute, weak, irresolute, undisciplined, sensual, obscene and proud. I was a mess."

No, the Thomas Merton whom the world remembers transcends all the biographical details that Merton himself defined in his far too premature autobiography, *Seven Storey Mountain*, and that time has laid bare. Instead, Thomas Merton became an archetype of Christian conscience and Christian search who took stock of his own life and so was a credible model for others who knew the struggles of life and its murky, slippery slopes. When everything else had withered and failed him, when the money became meaningless and the parties went dry, when the wandering became a curse and the license had lost its taste, Merton looked at last for meaning in life rather than for the satiating, the mundane. First, he found communism. Then he found philosophy. Then he found faith. Thomas Merton entered the Abbey of Gethsemane in Bardstown, Kentucky, at the age of twenty-six, on December 10, 1941, a convert of three years, a pacifist, and a very experienced young man. Not even the cloistered life would be business-as-usual for Thomas Merton.

Merton was a man with a monastic soul who brought new levels of meaning to the oldest elements of monastic life. Merton knew what had often been forgotten in monastic history: that monasticism is not about withdrawal; monasticism is about depth. From the silent center of a Cistercian monastery Merton became a commentator on the society around him. Removed from its motives, its profits, and its purposes, Merton saw them in the clear light of day and began to speak out about them. In *Seeds of Contemplation*, the first book he wrote after the publication of *Seven Storey Mountain*, the tone was set that would shape his contribution both to spirituality and to the social order. Where other spiritual writers emphasized the distance between things of the spirit and things of the world, Merton saw one as an attendant to the other. To Merton, the monk who presented himself in *Seven Storey Mountain* as a modern St. Augustine, debased in body and devoid of spirit, life nevertheless forever remained a sacrament to him, not a temptation. Rigorous asceticism and personal penance were not Merton's gift to the world; openness was. Merton was behind monastery walls, but his heart was porous and his sight was keen.

He was a prolific author, and his writings attracted people from every walk of life. Here was a monk who understood the world, and the world was waiting for him. "For myself, I have only one desire and that is the desire for solitude — to disappear into God, to be submerged in [God's] peace, to be lost in the secret of [God's] face," he wrote in *The Sign of Jonah,* but Merton was writing about what the world wanted to hear: the relationship of daily life to union with God. For too long, the world had been locked out of sanctity by the hierarchy of vocations. Monks and nuns, the theology taught, lived a higher life and were about the things of the spirit. The rest of the world was relegated to good works and penance for sins. Merton brought the two worlds together for the first time in this century. He never lost sight of humanity; he always saw it as the stuff of divinity.

But Thomas Merton was more than a social commentator with a spiritual lens. He was the sign that human struggle does not disqualify spiritual success. Thousands followed him into the faith; hundreds read his autobiography and found their own way to religious life as a result. Yet, Merton was not a monk's monk. He entertained guests; he had a correspondence to rival a corporate executive; he traveled around the world. Nevertheless, or even as a result perhaps, he did more to make monasticism a vibrant part of contemporary life than anyone else in his generation. It was not a contribution without cost.

He was silenced by his abbot. He was censored at every turn. His public popularity brought him continual interruptions. His desire to live the hermit's life within the confines of the monastery was denied him time after time. But none of it mattered. Over the years Merton, the social critic, the peacemaker, the contemplative, became the best known, the most influential monk in the modern world, despite his own struggles

with his vocation, despite his own erratic but persistent attempts to put his writing down.

Merton left three legacies: the Christian vocation to peacemaking, a respect for Eastern monasticism in the Western world, and a renewed understanding of the religious vocation. He was ahead of his time on all three issues. The United States was at war when he spoke for peace and nonviolence; the Far East was still a remote and mysterious place when he sought to bridge the gap between Eastern and Western meditation modes; religious life was in a state of universal decline and diminishment. Merton had a new vision for each.

With the world gone mad with the technologies of war and the churches blessing bombers and putting the flag of the nation in their sanctuaries, Merton wrote in *New Seeds of Contemplation:*

> The present war crisis is something we have made entirely for and by ourselves. There is in reality not the slightest logical reason for war, and yet the whole world is plunging headlong into frightful destruction, and doing so with the purpose of avoiding war and preserving peace! This true war-madness is an illness of the mind and spirit that is spreading with a furious and subtle contagion all over the world. Of all the countries that are sick, America is perhaps the most grievously afflicted. On all sides we have people building bomb shelters where, in case of nuclear war, they will simply bake slowly instead of burning quickly or being blown out of existence in a flash. And they are prepared to sit in these shelters with machine guns with which to prevent their neighbor from entering. This in a nation that claims to be fighting for religious truth along with freedom and other values of the spirit. Truly we have entered the "post-Christian era" with a vengeance. Whether we are destroyed or whether we survive, the future is awful to contemplate.

Eventually, Merton was "silenced" on political issues. But his voice had been heard. In spite of the classic commitment of Christians to the "just" war theory, Merton steadily, doggedly pulled the world back from the brink of the holy war theology to a whole new way of looking at the

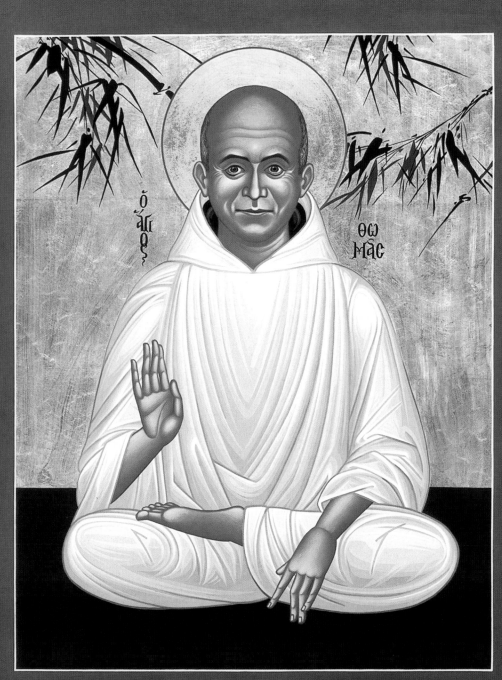

Ο ΑΓΙΟ ΘΩΜΑC

THOMAS MERTON

barbaric clash of highly computerized armies with the masses of unarmed and defenseless civilians who now bore the brunt of their governments' mad stabs at power. "What is the place of the Christian in all this?" he asked in an article in *The Catholic Worker* in 1961 as the Vietnam War began its terrible brew.

> Are Christians simply to fold their hands and resign ourselves for the worst, accepting it as the inescapable will of God....Or, worse still, should we take a hard-headed and "practical" attitude about it and join in the madness of the war makers, calculating how, by a "first strike," the glorious Christian West can eliminate atheistic communism for all time and usher in the millennium?...What are we to do? The duty of the Christian in this crisis is to strive with all our power and intelligence, with our faith, our hope in Christ, our love for God and humanity, to do the one task which God has imposed upon us in the world today. There can be no question that unless war is abolished the world will remain constantly in a state of madness and desperation in which, because of the immense destructive power of modern weapons, the danger of catastrophe will be imminent and probable at every moment everywhere. Unless we set ourselves immediately to this task, both as individuals and in our political and religious groups, we tend by our very passivity and fatalism to cooperate with the destructive forces that are leading inexorably to war. It is a problem of terrifying complexity and magnitude, for which the Church itself is not fully able to see clear and decisive solutions. Yet she must lead the way on the road to non-violent settlement of difficulties and toward the gradual abolition of war as the way of settling international or civil disputes. Christians must become active in every possible way.

Criticism of Merton accelerated on every side: from those patriots in the country for whom war was a solemn political loyalty test, from the board of Cistercian censors, from conservative Catholics. Merton was silenced on "political" issues, but, suddenly, the Peace Movement had a military chaplain of its own and there was another bell sounding in the tower of the church.

Merton struggled for years with the idea that his own vocation was to go deeper and deeper into prayer and meditation and silence where sight becomes clearer and life is stripped to its barest priorities. As the public pressures on him increased and the community restrictions intensified, Merton toyed with the idea of moving out of his Cistercian order, where life was lived in community, to the Camaldolese order, where monks lived in a common compound but in individual hermitages around a church for common prayer. "The singular advantage of such a life," Merton argued in *The Silent Life*, "is that it makes it possible for a pure contemplative life of real solitude and simplicity, without formalism and without rigid, inflexible prescriptions of minor detail, yet fully protected by spiritual control and by religious obedience." Merton's abbot, Dom James, knew what Merton failed to realize or chose to ignore: that Merton was now as important to the souls of many as he was to his own. Leaving Gethsemane, the abbot decided, was not good for Thomas Merton himself and it was not good for others either.

Merton stayed at Gethsemane. More than that, Merton began to explore the place of people and things in the development of the genuine spiritual life. He wrote in *Conjectures of a Guilty Bystander:*

> It is a glorious destiny to be a member of the human race, though it is a race dedicated to many absurdities and one which makes many terrible mistakes: yet, with all that, God...gloried in becoming a member of the human race. A member of the human race!...There is no way of telling people that they are all walking around shining like the sun....There are no strangers!...If only we could see each other [as we really are] all the time. There would be no more war, no more hatred, no more cruelty, no more greed....I suppose the big problem would be that we would fall down and worship each other....The gate of heaven is everywhere.

Merton's new understanding of the stuff of contemplation led him beyond the boundaries of the order and into the very center of the contemplative vocation. As wars raged and racism consumed the country and feminism began to critique the established order, Merton began to look for bridges across the human divide. He became more and more interested in the monasticism of the Eastern religions, reaching out always for the intangibles that transcend boundaries and races and denominations in favor of that one unity that sanctifies us all, humanity. At the Calcutta conference in October of 1967 Merton said to the Asian monks assembled there,

> The deepest level of communication is not communication, but communion. It is wordless. It is beyond words, and it is beyond speech, and it is beyond concept. Not that we discover a new unity. We discover an older unity. My dear brothers, we are already one. But we imagine that we are not. What we have to recover is our original unity. What we have to be is what we are.

Contemplation, Merton knew, was the key to experiencing that unity because contemplation, whatever its denominational origin, is simply coming to view life through the heart of God. It is coming to see the world as God sees the world. As one.

In an age when all of religious life itself was bursting apart at the seams, shedding one period of history, trying to become leaven in another, Merton began to live into the new model right before our eyes. Merton knew that the role of religious life in the modern world was to develop people of substance who were immersed in questions of social significance. Merton knew that religious life was not the fine art of maintaining monastic museums. On the morning of his death, Merton delivered his last public paper, "Marxism and Monastic Perspectives," to the Bangkok conference of Benedictine and Cistercian abbots. The monastic, he said, "is essentially someone who takes up a critical attitude toward the world and its structures...[saying] that the claims of the world are fraudulent."

Merton the man taught the world that the spiritual life is not the elimination of struggle; it is the sanctification of struggle. It is struggle transformed to wisdom.

Merton the monk taught the world that withdrawal is not of the essence of a holy life. The essence of a holy life is immersion in the spiritual and commitment to the significant.

Merton the contemplative taught the world that we know that we will have come to see God when we have come to see people as sacred.

Thomas Merton, man, monk, contemplative, is sign that the heights of human attainment are in the lowest of us. Thomas Merton, icon, sounds the voice of a creator who goes on caring.

CATHERINE of SIENA
Woman of Courage

As a Sufi story teaches, "There are those in winter who, calling themselves religious, say 'I shall not wear warm clothes. I shall trust in God's kindness to protect me from the cold.' But these people," the Sufi teach, "do not realize that the God who created cold has also given human beings the means to protect themselves from it."

The point, of course, is that we must not expect God to do for us what God means for us to do for ourselves. If there is any figure in history who is sign of that truth and who calls the entire Christian tradition over and over to learn the same lesson now it is surely Catherine of Siena. Mystic, theologian, religious recluse, she was also one of the most socially active, most publicly influential, and most theologically piercing women in the history of the church.

Catherine of Siena walked the cutting edge of life with an ease that dazzles the mind. When religious life for women was defined by cloister and depended on the common life for both its credibility and its legitimacy, Catherine of Siena ignored the demands of categories that did not work for her and turned an association of semi-cloistered widows into an alternative style of religious commitment. These women lived vowed lives alone in their homes and walked the streets of the city doing good for others—no matter who said that such a thing could not really be religious life at all. And in that act, she prefigured today's religious life for all the church to see.

When theology was the province of the men of the church alone, Catherine of Siena was spiritual director to one man after another, including her own confessor. In that act she claimed the spiritual humanity of women for ages to come.

When mysticism was veiled in mystery and wrapped in private ecstasies and personal devotions, Catherine's mysticism plagued her with the worries of the world and plunged her into the very center of life. And in that act she called religion out of privatism for all the pious to see.

When the role of women was not even an issue, Catherine made it one. In that act she raised the question that will not die for any of us.

When everything in the world around her was in chaos, in both church and state, Catherine refused to buy for herself an easy reprieve. She would not call the unhuman natural. She would not call what was wrong right, what was intolerable acceptable, what was bad good, what was oppressive God's will. Not even when it came from the highest ranks of the political order; not even when it came from the very center of the papacy. No, Catherine of Siena called the terrible terrible and the ungodly ungodly and in that act calls every century after her yet, still, and always, to do the same. Today, still, Catherine of Siena pours fire and ice into the human soul. She confronts us with what we dearly need even now if this church is to prosper and this world is to survive.

Ҥ ӑ҃лӏа ҟ҃атеρӏ҃на

ST. CATHERINE ⨍ SIENA

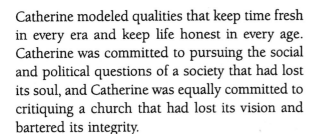 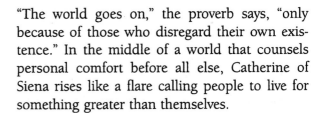

Catherine modeled qualities that keep time fresh in every era and keep life honest in every age. Catherine was committed to pursuing the social and political questions of a society that had lost its soul, and Catherine was equally committed to critiquing a church that had lost its vision and bartered its integrity.

Catherine had four qualities sorely needed in this day, too, if the twenty-first century is to hold more promise than burden for the little ones, the lost ones, the unloved ones of life. In the first place, Catherine of Siena was able to live beyond her natural inclinations. Catherine was not a child of the me-generation, not even in spiritual things. In fact, if there is anything that is capable of trapping us in selfishness, it is surely the spiritual life with its seductions of transcendence and righteousness and seclusion and holy indifference. Catherine of Siena, however, who had wanted with all her heart to be a hermit, gave up the solitude that could have seduced her into a false piety to follow God into the tabernacle of the world, into the pain and problems of the people around her, where the one who said, "Behold, I am with you all days," would surely be.

It is so easy to sink back into religion for its own sake, to leave business to the business people and politics to the politicians and poverty to the poor and the church to the clerics — and all in the name of a hidden God. But Catherine of Siena stands in mute conviction of the self-centeredness that masks as piety. She walked the streets with food for the hungry, clothes for the homeless, and money for the poor calling every religious generation after her out into the streets, up out of spiritual complacency and back into the real world. Catherine calls us now to walk where the people of God are still homeless, still forgotten, and still scourged, this time by the tax breaks of the wealthy and the militarism of the powerful and the platitudes of the pious who watch it all from their pews and their pulpits and say nothing, nothing, nothing at all.

"The world goes on," the proverb says, "only because of those who disregard their own existence." In the middle of a world that counsels personal comfort before all else, Catherine of Siena rises like a flare calling people to live for something greater than themselves.

In the second place, Catherine of Siena is a sign to the twenty-first century because she relied on insight where education failed. Her teaching was from the Holy Spirit. She went into the heart of God to see the world as God saw the world, and she spoke from the perspective of what was right rather than what was legal. It was certainly legal for the pope to send French legates to rule his Italian city-states, but it was not good for either the people or the church, and Catherine said so, and said so, and said so until the practice that almost destroyed the country and nearly devastated the credibility of the church had stopped.

In our time, too, they tell us that inhuman poverty in the midst of obscene affluence is normal, that the industrial slavery waged by First World corporations against Third World peoples is "development," that planned planetary destruction is a rational response to reasonable conflicts. They educate us to believe that what is legal is good, that what is male is best, that what is common is necessary. But education has clearly failed us where war is concerned and where women are concerned. Education is obviously not enough. Catherine of Siena teaches us to rely on insight again, to develop a clarity about God and a commitment to truth again.

In the third place, Catherine of Siena was a feminist cut out of the cloth of God. Literally. Catherine knew the place and role of women in society very well indeed. "How can I be of any use in the work of saving souls," she asked the Christ who called her in visions, "for I am a woman, and it is not seemly for my sex to try to teach men, or even to speak with them. Besides they take no notice of what we say." Obviously, Catherine knew the proper place for a woman in the universe. It was God who did not. It was the Jesus of her vision who responded:

All things are possible for God who has created everything from nothing. I know that you say this from humility, Catherine, but you must know that in these days pride has grown monstrously among men, and chiefly among those who are learned and think they understand everything. It was for this reason that at another period I sent out simple men who had no human learning, but were filled by me with divine wisdom and let them preach. Today, I have chosen unschooled women, fearful and weak by nature, but trained by me in the knowledge of the divine so that they may put vanity and pride to shame. If men will humbly receive the teachings I send them through the weaker sex I will show them great mercy, but if they despise these women they shall fall into even worse confusion and even greater agony.

Jesus had better not say those things ever again. The city of Siena may be one thing but the city of Rome and the chanceries of the world are totally another. The current theology dictates quite clearly that the world must beware the outrageous implications of the doctrine of creation and the theology of the Spirit that blows where it wills — even in women, even in the church. Yet because of those heretical words of Jesus, Catherine of Siena became spiritual mother, public figure, political prophet, Doctor of the Church. She read souls, guided priests, negotiated between city-states, chastised two popes, and became an emissary to the state from the Vatican. And she was always right and she never failed and she never quit.

It took attempt after attempt, letter after letter, protest after protest, but, finally, she brought the French pope out of his self-imposed political exile in French Avignon back to the See of Peter and the seat of the universal church. She saved the papacy from nationalism and chauvinism and deterioration of the soul of the church and the rot of church politics.

She called the rulers of Europe to be men rather than ruthless, adolescent bullies whose war games pitted the pitiful against the innocent. She held out for their measurement values greater than machismo and male power games. She commanded respect for women as well as for men, and she calls us to do the same.

She calls us to measure our world by standards beyond the worldly. She calls us to look at what's happening around us through the filter of the Gospel and to say what we see so that the conspiracy of silence that keeps the world in bondage to false assumptions, distorted traditions, and consuming hierarchies of power and profit may be forever shattered, unalterably dismantled, totally undone.

She calls men to recognize the God-given mission of women affirmed by Jesus, enshrined in the Gospels, and confirmed by the history of women in the church. She calls women to refuse rejections, to demand equality, to speak their spirituality, to give their God-given gifts, whether these gifts are called for or not, called holy or not, legitimated or not because no one, not even the church, has the right to deny the gifts of God or the God who works through the gifts of women.

Finally, and perhaps most important of all, Catherine of Siena was a patient prophet. She gave her entire life for truth and peace; she persisted for the long haul. She stood immovable in the midst of mayhem, and she never blinked. And, God knows, she met opposition everywhere: some people criticized her public ecstasies as religious ostentation, and others criticized her involvement in public affairs as unreligious. Some people called her travels worldly, and others called her steady, reckless, untiring commitment to the local poor extravagant. Some people criticized her virginity, and some people criticized her friendships with men. They criticized her commitment to the church, and they criticized her criticism of it. But they never, ever broke her spirit or deterred her work or confused her vision or diverted her path. None of them, not the family, not the city, not the rulers, not the churchmen, not even the "mantellate," the women of her own community whose silent, secret jealousies grew in proportion to her obvious greatness and cast shadows on the light that was in her. She prodded popes to cure the church of its corruption, provoked rulers to cure the city-states of their vulturous greed, protested in behalf of the people who were crucified by it all, and persisted and persisted and persisted. She never stopped, she never backed down, and she never left.

She was a voice, a warning, a torch when truth was dimmed and life was deceptive and days were dark. And she is a silent accuser of the lives of those now as well who, when they see the hungry and the homeless and the unemployed, say nothing in a country that has money aplenty for the things of war but little or nothing for the ways of peace. She is a voice of conscience to those who pride themselves on the fact that they have curtailed welfare for the poor, all the while increasing their tax welfare programs for the rich. She is a persistent spur to those who sit idly by while the West rapes the world and reaps those profits for itself. She is a perpetual pique to those who find nothing to fear in the loss of the ozone layer, the rain forests, the grazing lands, or the water of the world. She is a voice of judgment for those who have nothing to say about the rejection of women in a church that calls itself "one in Christ Jesus" and then leaves women out of its synods and out of its services and out of its sacraments in a sacramental church.

The life of Catherine of Siena is an icon of the God of Surprises, a thunderclap that vibrates through the life of each of us. Catherine of Siena calls across the centuries with frightening clarity. Catherine of Siena becomes a woman to be reckoned with again. As long as there are poor among us, Catherine of Siena is a woman to be reckoned with again. As long as there is war anywhere, then Catherine of Siena is a woman to be reckoned with again. As long as the church is more an institution than a vehicle of the Gospel, then

Catherine of Siena is a woman to be reckoned with again. As long as any woman anywhere is demeaned or diminished or dismissed out of hand as foolish or incompetent or lesser in the sight of God and little in the church, as long as anyone anywhere says a hostile and unholy "no" to women, then Catherine of Siena is a woman to be reckoned with again.

Catherine of Siena was a woman who suffered with the suffering in ways that most do not. She was a woman whose spiritual life exceeded the bounds of ecclesiastical law. She was a woman who refused to let womanhood be used as an argument against her. She was a woman who sought to create a religious life in her own home but was willing to leave it so that the world could become more a home and so that the church could become more religious.

Catherine of Siena was a woman whose life God flung across our sky to out-meteor, out-comet, out-star, and out-brighten every sick and squalid age to come, to touch and sear even yet, even now, even us, even here. We too must learn to go against the natural inclinations to buy peace at any price, and we must try even harder to derail the war mentality that makes the world poor. We too must learn to trust the insights of the Gospel when education fails to persuade the rich to care for the poor and calls that obscene insensitivity "the business cycle." We too must learn to claim Christian feminism when the designs of God for women are obstructed by the state in the name of law and by the church in the name of the will of God. We, too, must learn to be patient when the walls of poverty do not fall, when the wars for resources do not end, and the women of the world are wanted more for their domestic services than for their spiritual powers. Why? Because it is the measure of the things to which we give our allegiance that is the measure of ourselves.

Personal sacrifice, Gospel insight, Christian feminism, and patient prophetism is the legacy of Catherine of Siena to the twenty-first century.

JOAN of ARC
A Voice of Conscience

I t seems at first glance to be hardly the stuff of which contemporary sanctity is made. The story of Joan of Arc as we have known it is an almost mythical one, a fantasy of divine proportions. She was a peasant, a simple girl from the unsophisticated countryside, who took it upon herself to save the country when its leaders could not. She was impelled by the voices of St. Catherine of Siena, St. Margaret, and the Archangel Michael, she said, to follow the will of God. She was to liberate a city, lead an army, save a king, and free a nation from foreign control. The story seems remote, the model suspect, and voices from heaven not a common way of expressing contemporary spiritual insights or calls from God. At best, the story belongs to another age, hardly to ours.

With the English invading France at the height of the Hundred Years War, the city of Orleans under siege, and the Dauphin, the heir to the French throne, deprived of his rights to the throne, France was without a leader, without a resistance movement, and so without a nation. The fifteenth century was, Twain wrote, "the worst century since the Dark Ages." The country was about to lose its identity. The peasant population of France was being ground under foot

ЇѠ ÁΝ ΝΑ

JEANNE D'ARC

by a foreign power, their lands usurped, their villages destroyed, and their crops ruined. For them there was no recourse, no defense, no leadership at all.

Into the midst of this medieval tale comes a seventeen-year-old girl who, in the 1400s, dresses like a man, leads an army, raises the siege of Orleans, and provides France with a king. There, perhaps, the fantasy ends. In the end, Joan is captured by her English enemies and burned at the stake with the help of churchmen who consider her a heretic, label her a witch, and condemn her to death because of her refusal to denounce her voices as the church has commanded her to do.

It is a pathetic situation. The girl who, with the approval of French churchmen, risks her life to follow the voices of God within her is condemned by a different church court, which included another set of bishops, both English and French, and is burned by these judges for failing to be a faithful daughter of the church.

The relation of all that to sanctity in the twenty-first century seems at best obscure until little by little the local history is peeled away and the light is focused on the very human and very universal situation that underlies it. Joan is not remembered because she was a soldier in the service of a king. Joan is to be revered because she is a model of conscience development, a monument to the feminine relationship to God, and a breaker of the stereotypes that block the will of God for people.

Joan's problem was that she was caught between what clearly had to be done to right oppression in a system and the then present political will of the church. French theologians had found her stable and orthodox. The English bishops who tried her after her capture called her a witch and a heretic.

Joan was tried on seventy-two charges. The most serious ones were two: she dressed like a man,

and she refused to put the authority of the church before what her inner voices, her conscience, demanded.

George Bernard Shaw presents the situation clearly in his scene of the church trial before the English episcopal judges and Inquisitor. D'Estivet is the prosecutor; Ladvenu is a Dominican monk who believes in Joan and supports her. The assessors are the churchmen responsible for evaluating the evidence. They are totally hostile to Joan:

> JOAN: I am a faithful child of the Church. I will obey the Church—
>
> CAUCHON (*hopefully leaning forward*): You will?
>
> JOAN: — provided it does not command anything impossible.

The struggles of conscience over authority is a mighty one. All officialdom arrayed, however, cannot sway the young Joan. There are some things in life that belong to God alone, Joan implies — human life, human responsibility, and human will.

> THE INQUISITOR: If the Church Militant tells you that your revelations and visions are sent by the devil to tempt you to your damnation, will you not believe that the Church is wiser than you?
>
> JOAN: I believe that God is wiser than I; and it is God's commands that I will do.... If any Churchman says the contrary I shall not mind him: I shall mind God alone, whose command I always follow....
>
> JOAN: God must be served first.
>
> D'ESTIVET: Then your voices command you not to submit yourself to the Church Militant.
>
> JOAN: My voices do not tell me to disobey the Church; but God must be served first.
>
> CAUCHON: And you, and not the Church, are to be the judge?
>
> JOAN: What other judgement can I judge by but my own?

In every age governments tell people what is good for them and cloak the national good in

127

moral terms. Sometimes it is "Kill a Commie for Christ" that is preached; sometimes it is saturation bombing of whole regions that is called good in the name of "freedom" when what is really freed is oil. Sometimes it is gay bashing that is called godly. In every moment, Joan of Arc hears another voice and says "No."

> INQUISITOR: As to this matter of the man's dress. For the last time, will you put off that impudent attire, and dress as becomes your sex?

> JOAN: I will not.

> LADVENU: Can you suggest to us one good reason why an angel of God should give you such shameless advice?

> JOAN: Why, yes: what can be plainer common sense? I was a soldier living among soldiers. I am a prisoner guarded by soldiers. If I were to dress as a woman they would think of me as a woman; and then what would become of me? If I dress as a soldier they think of me as a soldier, and I can live with them as I do at home with my brothers....

Suddenly, Joan of Arc appears in the plain light of our own lives. She is a woman with a conscience. She is a woman with a mission. She is a woman who has been chosen by God for a man's job. She is a woman who is bold enough to claim that she has access to God and that God has outrageous plans for her. She is a woman who dares to confront the authorities of the time with a greater question than they are able or willing to handle. She is a woman who threatens the status quo. She is a woman.

She tells an inspired truth and leads a life consecrated to her God.

It is a sad story but a hopeful one. The church that condemned her is also the church that canonized her. She died for her truth, true, but others have lived better for it because of her.

In the life of Joan of Arc we see the God who works at will, outside the norms, despite the mores, in contrast to dying systems.

Joan of Arc is not simply the patron of France in times such as ours. Joan of Arc is patron of all those who hear the voice of God calling them beyond present impossibilities to the fullness of conscience everywhere.

Epilogue

An ancient Chinese proverb teaches: "If we stay on the road we are on we shall surely get where we are going." It is a sobering thought. This generation is on the road to ozone depletion, global poverty of unprecedented proportions, massive concentration of wealth and resources in the hands of a few, technological explosion, biological cataract, and theological upheaval if for no other reason than that new science demands a new dimension to old theologies. In the future, we cannot teach the concept of "taking dominion" of the Garden of Eden the way we have in the past or we stand to destroy the earth and ourselves with it. We cannot teach the sanctity of life without teaching the immorality of war. We cannot teach the notion of heaven without teaching the unknowns of quantum physics as components of the faith. In the face of a changing world, a shifting culture, a global perspective, we cannot teach the glories of man without teaching the equality of women. We cannot make tradition more important than ongoing revelation. We cannot use theology to obstruct thought, to deter human development, to make church a place rather than a people nor can we use the idea of "authority" to justify oppression.

There is no doubt about it: The twenty-first century will be a difficult and a dangerous one. Whatever shall propel us through it?

Old answers will not do it. Old politics will not do it. Old economics certainly will not do it. Old church cannot do it. This book says that only the image of those who have themselves bridged equally wide fissures of the past can give us the sight, give us the hope, give us the courage that it will take to face population increase, institutionalized greed, and theological decadence with aplomb.

This desert is our desert. This time is our time. This challenge is our challenge. This sin is our sin. It is we who hold the future in our hands.

We need a new image of God.

We need a new respect for the poor and exploited.

We need a new model of women.

We need a new kind of man.

We need new models of holy madness and wisdom and justice and fire.

We need new models of holiness.

We need a new kind of conscience and a new sense of God's righteous anger.

We need a commitment to non-force and a sense of gentle strength.

We need to look eye to eye into the Face of Truth and come brow to brow with the pre-science of God and stand face to face with the heart of God.

We need exemplars of all these things — or how shall we ever come to them ourselves, in our time, at our age, with our great needs?

We need to stand up together, to link arms with the Great Ones of the past in order to find within ourselves the Great Heart it will take to shape the future.

May the simple people here who have walked through time before us — lay and religious, male and female, Christian and non-Christian — lead us together into the mind of God.

Then, together, may we find a passion for life and become ourselves, for the next generation, fragments of the face of God.

Thank you for being the way.

JOAN CHITTISTER, OSB
ROBERT LENTZ

Recommended Readings

Introduction

Woodward, Kenneth. *Making Saints: How the Catholic Church Determines Who Becomes a Saint, Who Doesn't and Why.* New York: Simon & Schuster, 1990.

Pedro Arrupe

Arrupe, Pedro, S.J. *Witnessing to Justice.* Vatican City: Pontifical Commission, Justice and Peace, 1972.

"Pedro Arrupe, S.J., 1907–1991." *America* 164 (February 16, 1991): 139–174.

Baal Shem Tov

Newman, Louis, ed. *The Hasidic Anthology: Tales and Teachings of the Hasidim.* New York: Schocken Books, 1963.

Benedict

Gregory the Great, Pope. *Dialogues.* Vol. 2, *Life and Miracles of St. Benedict.* Collegeville, Minn.: St. John's Abbey Press, 1949.

Catherine of Siena

Turpin, Joanne. *Women in Church History: Twenty Stories for Twenty Centuries.* Cincinnati, Ohio: St. Anthony Messenger Press, 1989.

Dorothy Day

Ellsberg, Robert, ed. *Dorothy Day: Selected Writings.* Maryknoll, N.Y.: Orbis Books, 1992.

Forest, Jim. *Love Is the Measure: A Biography of Dorothy Day.* Maryknoll, N.Y.: Orbis Books, 1986.

Jordan, Patrick. "Dorothy Day: Still a Radical." *Commonweal* (November 1985): 665–69.

Charles de Foucauld

Lepetit, Charles. *Two Dancers in the Desert: The Life of Charles de Foucauld.* Maryknoll, N.Y.: Orbis Books, 1983.

Six, Jean-François. *Witness in the Desert: The Life of Charles de Foucauld.* New York: Macmillan Co., 1965.

Francis and Clare

Armstrong, Regis J., OFM, and Ignatius C. Brady, OFM, trans. *Francis and Clare: The Complete Works.* New York: Paulist Press, 1982.

Dennis, Marie, et al. *St. Francis and the Foolishness of God.* Maryknoll, N.Y.: Orbis Books, 1993.

Peterson, Ingrid J. *Clare of Assisi: A Biographical Study.* Quincy, Ill.: Franciscan Press, 1993.

Gandhi

Ashe, Geoffrey. *Gandhi.* New York: Stein and Day, 1969.

Fisher, Louis, ed. *The Essential Gandhi: His Life, Work, and Ideas.* New York: Vintage Books, 1962.

Merton, Thomas, ed. *Gandhi on Non-Violence.* New York: New Directions, 1964.

Shirer, William L. *Gandhi: A Memoir.* New York: Simon & Schuster, 1979.

Hildegard of Bingen

Bowie, Fiona, and Oliver Davies, eds. *Hildegard of Bingen: Mystical Writings.* New York: Crossroad, 1990.

———. *Hildegard of Bingen.* The Classics of Western Spirituality. New York: Paulist Press, 1990.

Dreyer, Elizabeth. *Passionate Women: Two Medieval Mystics.* New York: Paulist Press, 1989.

Fox, Matthew, O.P. *Illuminations of Hildegard of Bingen.* Santa Fe, N.M.: Bear & Co., 1985.

Newman, Barbara. *Sister of Wisdom.* Berkeley: University of California Press, 1987.

Franz Jagerstatter

Zahn, Gordon. *In Solitary Witness.* Springfield, Ill.: Templegate Publishers, 1986.

Joan of Arc

Michelet, Jules. *Joan of Arc.* New York: A. L. Burt Co., 1900.

Shaw, George Bernard. *St. Joan.* New York: Penguin Books, 1951.

John XXIII

John XXIII, Pope. *Journal of a Soul.* Trans. Dorothy White. New York: Signet Books, 1964.

Michaels, Louis. *The Stories of Pope John XXIII.* Springfield, Ill.: Templegate, 1964.

Mother Jones

Atkinson, Linda. *Mother Jones: The Most Dangerous Woman in America.* New York: Crown Publishers, 1978.

Fetherling, Dale. *Mother Jones, The Miner's Angel.* Carbondale: Southern Illinois University Press, 1974.

Steel, E. M., ed. *The Speeches and Writings of Mother Jones.* Pittsburgh: University of Pittsburgh Press, 1988.

Julian of Norwich

Jantzen, Grace M. *Julian of Norwich: Mystic and Theologian.* New York: Paulist Press, 1988.

Julian of Norwich. *Revelations of Divine Love.* Trans. Clifton Wolters. London: Penguin Books, 1971.

Julian of Norwich: Showings. New York: Paulist Press, 1978.

Llewelyn, Robert. *All Shall Be Well.* New York: Paulist Press, 1982.

———, ed. *Julian, Woman of Our Day.* Mystic, Conn.: Twenty-Third Publications, 1987.

Underhill, Evelyn. *Cambridge Medieval History.* Vol. 7, ed. Tanner et al. Cambridge: Cambridge University Press, 1949.

Martin Luther King

Abernathy, Ralph David. *And the Walls Came Tumbling Down.* New York: Harper & Row, 1989.

Bennett, Lerone, Jr. *What Manner of Man.* Chicago: Johnson Publishing Co., 1964.

Cartwright, John H., ed. *Essays in Honor of Martin Luther King, Jr.* Evanston, Ill.: Garrett Evangelical Theological Seminary, 1971.

Oates, Stephen B. "Trumpet of Conscience." *American History Illustrated* 23 (April 1988): 18-27.

Bartolomé de Las Casas

Hanke, Lewis. *All Mankind Is One.* DeKalb: Northern Illinois University Press, 1974.

Las Casas, Bartolomé de. *The Devastation of the Indies.* New York: Seabury Press, 1974.

Richard, Pablo. "1492: God's Violence and the Future of Christianity." *International Review of Mission* 82, no. 325 (January 1993): 87-95.

Sanderlin, George, ed. *Witness: The Writings of Bartolomé de Las Casas.* Maryknoll, N.Y.: Orbis Books, 1992.

Sevilla-Casas, Elias. *Western Expansion and Indigenous Peoples.* Chicago: Mouton Publishers, 1977.

Martin of Tours

McNeil, John T. "Asceticism versus Militarism in the Middle Ages." *Church History* 5 (March 1935): 3-28.

Thomas Merton

Forest, Jim. *Living with Wisdom: A Life of Thomas Merton.* Maryknoll, N.Y.: Orbis Books, 1991.

McDonald, Thomas P., ed. *Through the Year with Thomas Merton.* Garden City, N.Y.: Image Books, 1985.

Merton, Thomas. *Conjectures of a Guilty Bystander.* New York: Doubleday, 1965.

———. *The Non-Violent Alternative.* Rev. ed. of *Thomas Merton on Peace.* Ed. Gordon Zahn. New York: Farrar, Straus & Giroux, 1980.

———. *A Passion for Peace: The Social Essays.* Ed. William H. Shannon. New York: Crossroad, 1995.

Oscar Romero

Brockman, James R. *Romero: A Life.* Maryknoll, N.Y.: Orbis Books, 1990.

Dear, John, S.J. *Oscar Romero and the Nonviolent Struggle for Justice.* Erie, Pa.: Benet Press, Pax Christi, USA, 1981.

Erdozain, Plácido. *Archbishop Romero.* Maryknoll, N.Y.: Orbis Books, 1980.

Sobrino, Jon. *Archbishop Romero: Memories and Reflections.* Maryknoll, N.Y.: Orbis Books, 1990.

Rumi

Barks, Coleman, and Robert Bly, eds. and trans. *Rumi: Night and Sleep.* Cambridge, Mass.: Yellow Moon Press, 1981.

Moyne, John, and Coleman Barks, trans. *Open Secret: Versions of Rumi.* Putnam, Vt.: Threshold Books, 1984.

Whinfield, E. H., ed. and trans. *The Triumphal Sun: A Study of the Works of the Jaloloddin Rumi.* 1978.

Edith Stein

Bordeaux, Henry. *Edith Stein: Thoughts on Her Life and Times.* Trans. Donald Gallagher and Idella Gallagher. Milwaukee: Bruce Publishing Co., 1959.

Gelber, J., and Romanus Leuven, eds. *The Collected Writings of Edith Stein.* Vol. 2. Trans. Freda Mary Ober. Washington, D.C.: ICS Publications, 1987.

Herbstrith, Waltrud. *Edith Stein: A Biography.* Trans. Bernard Bonowitz. San Francisco: Harper & Row Publishers, 1985.

Kateri Tekakwitha

Katarine Kekakwitha: The Lily of the Mohawks. The Position of the Historical Section of the Sacred Congregation of Rites. New York: Fordham University Press, 1940.

Sargent, Daniel. *Catherine Tekakwitha.* New York: Longmans, Green and Co., 1940.

Thwaites, R. G., ed. *Jesuit Relations and Allied Documents.* 73 vols. Cleveland, 1896-1901.

Teresa of Avila

Kavanaugh, Kieran, OCD, and Otilio Rodriguez, OCD. *Teresa of Avila: The Interior Castle.* New York: Paulist Press, 1979.

Levack, Brian P. *The Witch-Hunt in Early Modern Europe.* New York: Longman, 1987.

Lincoln, Victoria. *Teresa: A Woman.* Albany: State University of New York Press, 1984.

University Martyrs

"Grave Thoughts: A Conversation with Ignacio Ellacuría." *New Republic* 201, no. 24 (March 1989).

"Guilt in El Salvador: Demonizing D'Aubuisson." *Nation* 248 (May 8, 1989): 524.

Sobrino, Jon, *Companions of Jesus: The Jesuit Martyrs of El Salvador.* Maryknoll, N.Y.: Orbis Books, 1990.

Simone Weil

Ignatieff, Michael. "The Limits of Sainthood (Simone Weil)." *New Republic* 202 (June 18, 1990): 25-40.

Weil, Simone. *Waiting for God.* San Francisco: Harper & Row, 1951.

———. *Gravity and Grace.* London, Routledge, Kegan, Paul Publishers.